Liberation

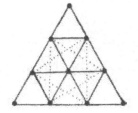

Father ~ beginning Teaching at The Source
1969

ANY PART OF THIS BOOK MAY BE REPRODUCED WITHOUT PERMISSION OF THE "AUTHOR". THE WORD OF GOD CANNOT BE COPYRIGHTED.

This was written by Father in the early 1970's, when The Source Family was still very young. This book is now being re-printed by the Source Foundation. The original text may be used – as Father wished – by anyone. The "Update" part of the book may not be copied without permission and is protected by copyright.

Published by:
"The Source"
8301 Sunset Blvd
Los Angeles, California
(in the early 1970's)

Re-published by:
The Source Foundation
PO Box 679
Kilauea, Hawaii
USA

6th printing – Copied from "FATHER'S" original
2004

This dedication was made by Jim / Father to his Spiritual Father, the Yogi. This re-print is dedicated to "Our" Earthly Spiritual Father . . .
   ~ Father / Father Yod / Ya Ho Wha ~

DEDICATED TO:

My beloved Father; the last of the Great Masters, Maharaji Yogi Bhajan.

The dawning New Age when every flesh father will also be an Earthly Spiritual Father, thus bringing to a timely end the necessity for a Middle man between man and his God.

The Great Saints and Sages of the past who are among us, now recognizable by their hair.

My beautiful courageous disciples who have found their way back to "The Source."

"Seek for him who is to give thee birth, in the Hall of Wisdom, the Hall which lies beyond, wherein all shadows are unknown, and where the Light of Truth shines with unfading glory."

Introduction

There is no "authors name" in this Book. There are two reasons: The Author is just a servant of God . . . . so cannot be said to be "The Author". The other reason is that this is the Age when some will stop relating to personalities, and begin to relate to "TRUTH". If the contents of this Book sound like Truth to you, then you really "knew" it already. The Master can only "pluck" the cords that are already "there". What you "flash" on is what you have Karmically earned to "hear" . . . .

Be forewarned that the contents are "very heavy" and are for the very few. Some will immediately see the TRUTH of these revelations . . . Others will have seeds planted which will sprout at a later date. Either way is "right". All are where they should be . . . . All are being inexorably pulled back to "The Source". Some a little in advance of others, but ALL must sooner or later return from "Whence they came." This is the Law . . . . and it does not matter whether you want to go or not . . . . . You must obey, sooner or later, and the sooner the better.

Life is a "school" . . . You are here to learn your lessons, for that you need the "Last Teacher". The Earthly Spiritual Father gives his Love and Wisdom to All, but All do not make equal use of it. <u>The Father can do nothing if the Son feels he is grown</u>. Many Spiritual Children today are caught in the trap of Spiritual ego. The reason being that the "truth" which they have, whereas "incomplete", still places them "head and shoulders" above their brothers and sisters who are temporarily caught in a dead spiritual Vibration. The only hope in this life for these Spiritually precocious children is for them to realize, through exposure to "right information" that they are still . . . . after all, Spiritual infants, in spite of their age, or ego inflating comparisons with the herd, and to seek the Wisdom of an Earthly Spiritual father.

Try to keep in mind that every Spiritual advance has been resisted by the majority of mankind of the time. Only a few have ever been ready each time the Force behind Evolution exerted itself. Who cannot feel the "pressure" today? Those who do not "get their act together" within a very short time will be found in hospital beds or running crazy in the streets.

In Every Age God appears in a different form and under a different name . . . . but always the same God, "for the protection of the innocent, I am born from age to age". For those who can "see" Him it will not matter what "hell" may break out around them . . . . They are held safe in the bosom of the Father. They have learned their "lessons" and so can, at WILL, pass on to another "grade".

Few will be able to respond to the prevailing Vibration of this time, because their Vibration is ill prepared to withstand the Power of It . . . . But those few will become the World Saviors. Many will learn that the Spiritual experience of the former Great Saints and Sages was not unique . . . and they too will have the same illumination. This is the Age when there will not be just "ONE" World Savior . . . but many. And these "many" are but a prelude to the time when ALL will be as God, and the "Sixth Day" will burst with all its splendor over the Earth, and Man and God will be as One . . . . And there will be no difference between men. You are now in the Cusp of this Age . . . . The so called "Golden Age" also known as "The Age of Aquarius".

All Birth is painful . . . . There is no birth that is not preceded by "pain" . . . . . . to practice and live by the revelations within this book is going to bring "pain" at first, to those who have the Strength to Master, finally, their senses . . . . But it is only difficult at first. Keep your goal in mind, and gain strength from knowing that all the Great Liberated Souls have walked the same Path which you now are on. You are not alone . . . . . Unseen forces are at work everywhere today seeking to aid those who have, "entered the stream". You have but to "enter" to make their presence felt. Those who are afraid to enter . . . . . those who are too timid to enter, and cool their weary souls . . . . . stand to perish from the heat. Most must still learn from life . . . . . few have the capacity to learn from a Teacher and avoid the experience. Life teaches with a "big stick" as many of you know. The Easy Way . . . . the gentle way . . . . . is to hear the Truth of "The Last Teacher" and then act upon it, and so avoid the experience of the painful karma.

Before most can do this, they must undergo the final disillusionment, the final humiliation, the final financial loss, before they are ready for the wisdom of the Earthly Spiritual Father.

So now my Loved Ones, turn within and listen for the voice of the Soul, and seek the light of the Spirit. You have them both within you . . . why seek further for that which can never reach you from the outside?

Kill in yourself all memory of past experiences . . . . Look not behind, the past is gone, and was but necessary to bring you to the place where you now are. Flee from the "Hall of Learning". Books and "Masters" are but necessary during your probation . . . . do not linger else your soul be trapped in the deceptive light, and perish like a moth attracted to the midnight flame. You cannot travel on the Path until you have become the Path itself . . . without movement does one travel on this Path.

Nothing that you have experienced in all of your past lifetimes is "lost" to you. All of the accumulated wisdom of age after age is securely locked within your subconscious mind. The contents of that part of your mind were earned by you at the greatest possible cost. If you could recall the lifetime after lifetime you were tortured and put to death for your Spiritual beliefs, you would see clearly that the blood shed, and the tortures born by the "recorded" Saints were your own. He who, "died for your sins" was you, my loved ONE. And always, it was because of you that the level of humanity's awareness was raised to a new vibration. Yes, your present level of Spiritual awareness was gained through blood, sweat and tears. The wisdom earned is within you . . . . . . Locked securely within your subconscious mind . . . . . . and only YOU have the key. But for most the key has grown rusty in the lock and will not turn. To shed the LIGHT which dissolves all impediments is the purpose of this book. Your Soul crying for final release has been heard, and the very Universe's attention is focused upon the Planet Earth.

There is about to be a Great New Birth in the

World, and the Universe HOLDS ITS BREATH. Come the time of "delivery", and the Universe will INHALE the AH sound of God . . . . . . And Peace and LOVE will reign once more in the World.

YOU who will first master yourself by practicing the "code of conduct" necessary to achieve LIBERATION as revealed within this BOOK, will stand as MASTERS of this Planet, unaffected by all that goes on about you, for YOU will be THE SOURCE of new LIFE for ALL. The next Great Spiritual Vibration will EMANATE FROM YOU ! Your Soul sings in its chrysalis with anticipation. The last enemy, DEATH, will be conquered . . . . . . You will be LIBERATED while living.

The Ten Commandments
For The Age of Aquarius

I "Obey and live by the Teachings of your Earthly Spiritual Father"

II "Love your Earthly Spiritual Father more than yourself"

III "Harm not one of your body parts either by neglect, food, drink or knife"

IV "Allow each vibration to complete its own cycle without interference"

V "Possess nothing that you do not need, and share all that you have"

VI "The man and his woman are one, let nothing separate them"

VII "Squander not your creative force in lust, but come together only when the three vibrations of the physical, mental and emotional are in harmony with Spiritual Love"

VIII "Each morning join your vibration with the ascending currents of the Universal Life Energy, using the method your Earthly Spiritual Father has taught you"

IX "Do every act energetically, intelligently, truthfully and lovingly"

X "When these Commandments are mastered, leave the house of your Earthly Spiritual Father and do the work of your Heavenly Father"

THE WORD . . . . . .

"Obey and live by The Teachings of Your Earthly Spiritual Father"

You are the end result of millions of years of evolution. If you could remember for a moment the suffering you have gone through to reach your present stage of development, you would be overcome with grief from the memory, and regret, over your past lives. This Vehicle, which your Soul now occupies, is The Father's most precious gift to you, for by which you have an opportunity to Learn your final lessons, "Burn up" your "Karma", and achieve Liberation. You who are reading this have "entered" the stream. For you there is no going back. The Father is calling out to His Own, and the Power of His Love, operating through the Great Law of Attraction, cannot be ignored. Those who, in this, the Cusp period of the Age of Aquarius, ignore the "pull" will suffer in the Hands of time. The effects of their causes will be very hard, with little time lapse between the Cause and Effect. To spare you the pain. To remove the heavy karmic sheaths which now

Liberation

hide the Light of the Spirit within you, to free your Soul, to introduce you to the I AM within, is the reason for the First Commandment.

By the Obeying, and Living, of the Teachings of The Earthly Spiritual Father, you do not incur any new negative Karma. The Soul is then free from any additional burdens upon it, and aided by the light of the Spirit within, will finally free itself from its encasement. It cannot do this if you live in duality, and as fast as you gain help from a Spiritual truth, you cancel the effect with a negative cause.

There are those who have found a little spiritual truth, and they feel that, that which they have is all. And they are right. It is all for them, and they should not be judged. They are where they have arrived Karmically in their evolution, and they are reaping what they have sown. Some are fanatic, some are Lazy, but all are exactly where they have been able to evolve to, and there is no blame. But there are those who, regardless of age, recognize within themselves that they are Spiritual Children . . . these are the ones who are ready for the

Liberation

wisdom of the Father. On the earth level, as an infant, should your father of the flesh tell you not to touch the hot stove, and you persist, you get your fingers burnt . . . . on the spiritual level, the same law of Cause and Effect is operating, so now you understand why this commandment must be First. Some in their Ego will think that, "I in my ego", am saying this. It has always been so, No World Savior has ever escaped condemnation and ridicule, for they all were mirrors for those who beheld them, but this is the Age when there will not be just one Savior . . . . there will be many.

Your Earthly Spiritual Father will be the one you recognize as such, but to avoid your making a "mistake" in the choosing, know that He must have the following qualifications:

One: His Spiritual Truths are not for sale. Freely were they given to Him, and Freely are they given to You. The Earthly Spiritual Father does not need the nickels and dimes of his children. The Heavenly Father-Mother provides all that He needs. Beware of those who charge for their teachings, some flagrantly, others disguised.

Liberation

They have fallen into the Last Trap of the Holy Man, Spiritual Ego and Power.

These men can speak "Beautiful Truths" which confuse you in the light of their actions. Know that God does not dry up any channel available to Him. All can be learned from, on many different levels. The "heavier" ones are the greatest Liberators, inasmuch when the final disillusionment comes, there is no place else for the "chela" to go. Where is he to go? To another "Master"? Those who commit this Spiritual "error" will find themselves on a Spiritual treadmill going in a circle which never ends. Those who find themselves completely at a loss, will finally turn within and "Listen to the Voice of the Soul and seek the Light of the Spirit". These are the little ones who are ready for the wisdom of the Earthly Spiritual Father.

Two: He will always be available to you. He lives for you, and loves you. Your problems are His problems. There is always "time" for you.

Three: He will always speak truth to you, no matter what the circumstances. He is not bound by any attachment, and it doesn't matter if you

Liberation

have a million dollars or one, He will never "sugar coat" or evade the hard truth. He will risk losing you rather than spare you a pain if it is for your own good.

Four: He will never show partiality . . . . all are his children, and all are equally "valuable" in His eyes.

Five: Finally He will always Love you . . . . no matter what the circumstances. There is NOTHING that he has not done. There is no Earthly experience He has not had either in this, or past lives . . . . . how then could He ever condemn or judge you? He is "shock proof". He understands ALL so He can forgive ALL. But there is never anything really to forgive. For there is no "evil" in the world . . . . there is only ignorance. So now, my Loved Ones, think well over these words and when you realize the Great Truth revealed herein you are ready for the next Commandment.

*"Love your Earthly Spiritual
Father, more than yourself"*

The second commandment is most difficult to understand by those who have not seen the wisdom in the first Commandment.

Those who have the "Spiritual consciousness" necessary to accept the First Commandment need not concern themselves with the making of an "effort" to "obey" the Second Commandment . . . . For the Love will come naturally. On the Earth level, the son is like the father. This occurs because the love between them transcends self. On the Spiritual level, by the transference of self love, to the Earthly Spiritual Father, you open yourself to His Truth. Before a vessel can be filled it must be empty. Similarly, before you can be filled with the "Light of the Spirit" all ego, all sense of self must go. The child "loves and "obeys" unquestioningly and without a thought, because he is in a relatively pure state of evolvement.

You as a Spiritual Child experience these same feelings and emotions through your

Liberation

"involvement", so actually this Second commandment is more in the light of realization, which occurs to all on the Path, and is presented in this proper place as an explanation, rather than a Command . . . . For Love cannot be commanded. But, on the other hand, should be understood with wisdom, and valued as the Greatest Gift.

All have loved, and been hurt. Know my Loved Ones that true love is beyond the capacity to injure, and that what you have experienced, and thought was Love, was merely to lead you to where you are now. True love, "takes the pain of another". Unless a "love" can do this, it is not a love. It can be a "need", a "lust", etc., but not LOVE. True love endureth all things, and is patient. The two qualities the Spiritual aspirant stands most in the need of . . . to become these virtues . . . . you have but to give them.

"Harm not one of your body parts, either by neglect, food, drink, or knife"

If You have been able to "get past" the first Two commandments you are ready for this, The Third Commandment, which begins work in earnest upon Yourself. Understand this . . . . now and for always. It is ALL for You. Some will have difficulty with this realization because their past experiences have made them suspicious and skeptical, but never mind . . . . . All must come to this realization sooner or later, and the sooner the better. In your ignorance many of you have done great harm to your physical, mental and emotional bodies. But all is well, and everything you have experienced served a purpose. No "injury" is beyond repair as long as there is life. The "secrets" you will learn will enable you to bring new life into every cell and speed up the rejuvenating process of the body to a point where in some cases, the body remakes itself not on the average, "of once every seven years", but every two years! But later for this.

Liberation

The commandment says . . . . "Your body parts", for you are not this body, but you have been living in it as if you were. You have allowed it to master you. Now, begin to Master it. The Body makes a beautiful slave but a terrible master, for it is insatiable. The more you give it the more it wants, even to its own detriment. Past "pleasures" are remembered, and encores sought, and found, until you find yourself in one endless round of sensual gratification with the resulting loss of mental and physical health, not to mention peace of mind, happiness, and contentment. Before the external can be mastered, the internal must be mastered. This body . . . this mind of yours . . . must be brought under control. We do this by KNOWING what is best . . . and then acting upon it. ALL knowledge is useless unless it is acted upon. You will find that the reward is well worth any effort, and that every effort has its reward. This is so to encourage you to continue, and to remove any doubts that you are on the right path.

". . . . either by neglect . . . . " As the House

Liberation
for the Soul, the body should be kept clean, and the proper materials provided for its growth, maintenance and repair. It must be put to sleep at the best time to recuperate fully.

Every part of your body has a function, from the hair on your head, to the tonsils and appendix. I mention these organs for they are the most neglected and misunderstood. There is never an excuse for being dirty. Cleanliness of body and clothes shows self respect. You would not expect a King to come and sit in a dirty hut, so do not expect the Light of the Father to enter an unclean Temple. All colors are beautiful, but the wearing of white is most appropriate for all on the Path, for not only is white the highest vibration, but if there is a "spot" it shows. Undisguised cleanliness should be your presentation to the world.

God made us perfect . . . . if you can fix this Great Truth in your mind, you will begin to understand that everything in the body must have a purpose, and you will begin to form a basis for your Spiritual growth. Of all God's

Liberation

gifts, the hair has been the most abused and misunderstood. Like all organs of the body it has two functions: a primary and a secondary purpose. First, your hairs are your "Cosmic Roots" by which you pull into, and feed your body from the great reservoir of Universal Life Energy, Strength and Wisdom. (The allegorical story of Samson in the Bible told the wise this) Just as the tree sends its roots deep into the soil for its nutrients, man's hair draws into himself the life substance necessary for his well being and happiness. Some men, you will say, have achieved LIBERATION who cut their hair or shaved their heads . . . . ARE YOU SURE? Before deciding this issue, wait until you yourself achieve your goal, and then look down from your great height with the "eyes" you will have then . . . . you may see things differently.

The secondary function of the hair, which science just now is beginning to discover, is to provide the body with vitamin "D". Have you ever wondered about the fact that Vitamin "D" is almost non-existent in our food supply? There is some in dairy products, but not enough

Liberation

to meet the daily body requirements. So where is this precious vitamin to come from? The HAIR! In each of the approximately one hundred and Thirty thousand hairs on the head there are "little Vitamin "D" manufacturing plants" in every cell. The longer the hair . . . . the more cells . . . the more Vitamin D manufactured for the body. Few today have "seen the beauty, strength and grace of which the body is capable". Do you doubt what I am saying? Then be patient a few years until you see the "offspring" of these beautiful children with hair today!

All that is necessary to activate the chemical process necessary to make Vitamin "D" is the ultra-violet rays of the Sun playing upon the hair . . . just as all that is necessary for a tree to obtain its full height and beauty is the rays of the Sun dancing among its leaves. It all knew this simple truth (along with the other truths of diet . . . for all work as ONE unit) there would be no tuberculosis, or any of the other degenerative diseases plaguing mankind today, which medical science is at such a loss to account for. But we are not concerned with

Liberation

disease here . . . . we are concerned with health. Allopathic medicine had better cease it myopic approach to "health" and begin to work forward from the cradle, instead of backward from the grave . . . . . or the nutritionist of today will become the "Doctor" of tomorrow . . . . . and the "Doctor" of today will be limited in his service to the "patching" of injured bodies. In which capacity I have the greatest respect for modern "medicine". It is encouraging to see the many "lay", rugged individuals who are taking the responsibility of their health into their own hands . . . . where it belongs.

Man is "Sun" . . . . . constant . . . . strong. He needs the added protection of hair upon his face. Woman is "Moon" . . . . . reserved . . . . changing . . . . dependent. Her face is free of hair. Not only does man, by shaving, do a great injustice to himself . . . . He renders his face effeminate! Esthetically, man's hair is his natural adornment. It expresses his unique personality, adds dignity and beauty to his face, and marks the softer graces, and exquisite qualities of Woman by the lack of it. Thousand of the Great Saints and Sages of the past

Liberation

Piscean Age are reincarnating today, much to the alarm of a sick society. As of now, few of these beautiful young people with Hair realize just who they are . . . . or why they have come. But they are beginning to know. All over the land is dawning a new awareness. A great Spiritual awakening can be felt. All this has been viewed as "senseless" rebellion by those who resist change. But change is inevitable . . . there can be no evolution without change. Few understand these children. They are the first drops of rain that precede the monsoon. They herald the coming of the New Age. That day when "the Gods shall walk the earth" and there shall be no difference between the Father and the Son. Most of the little ones involved do not understand what it is that "drives" them, and Society, (as usual) sees only the outer "appearances" and "judges" (as usual) accordingly.

Liberation

Know all Ye who read this . . . . that these Children are the Salt of the Earth, that they are the true Children of God. It is true that many are "playing in the mud". But just as the Lotus grows in the mud . . . . this is merely a stage of their Spiritual Evolution . . . . so let them play . . . . Let them exhaust themselves in the "Maya". Many will perish . . . . just as the first drops of rain disappear into the dry earth unseen. Those who survive, will become the World Saviors. The next Great Spiritual Leadership for the World is to come from the West . . . . according to Ancient prediction. Who Society now calls "Hippies" will lead them. There is no birth unless preceded by "pain". All growth is painful . . . .Those who have suffered the, "final disillusionment" are ready to hear the words of the, "Earthly Spiritual Father". Until then . . . play on . . . play hard . . . get it all out. The day is coming very soon my Loved Ones when you will raise your arms to God in despair and cry out, "Oh God! There must be something else!" No prayer goes unheard . . . . No plea goes ignored. At that time the "unseen forces" will

Liberation

come to your assistance and through the UNLIMITED CHANNELS will flow what YOU need.

.... "food, drink" .... under this part of The Third Commandment we include any substance taken into the body through the mouth. In the ancient Upanishads, God's oldest known Scriptural communication to man, we read that one of the most important things for man to do on the Path is to eat what they called then: Satvic foods. In the recently discovered "Dead Sea Scrolls", God's latest communication to man by scripture (found in 1957 .... about the time of the advent of the "Hippie"), we read that the first step to God Realization is to "Clean up the Temple", by fasting and the eating of Natural Foods eaten in season without "benefit" of fire. All foods should be eaten in a natural state, and RAW. Some still feel that the discovery of the Dead Sea Scrolls accidentally coincided with the tremendous interest in Food today. Nothing "happens" without purpose.

Modern Nutritional Scientists substantiate the Truths found in the Dead Sea Scrolls with their

Liberation

"discovery" of the elusive "enzyme". It was found that the enzyme was absolutely vital to the "life" of the food properties locked within the food of Man, and that any heat above the body temperature (just as revealed in the Dead Sea Scrolls) would destroy the enzyme. If man only knew and understood the Law of perfection prevailing throughout all of Nature, He would not have the effrontery to assume that "he" could improve upon God's Work. If our Creator wanted us to eat "cooked food" He would have provided some sort of heat force field which the food would have to pass through before we ate it. So the cooking of food stands today as the greatest single crime that man has committed against his own health.

Running a very close second is man's use of chemical additives to his food supply. By so doing he burdens his eliminative system with a "foreign" substance with which, in all its millions of years of evolution, it has no experience . . . . so the body eliminates what it can, and the rest it stores and treats the same way it would the fat soluble vitamins . . . . It stores these poisonous

Liberation

chemicals in its own fatty tissue! The result of this is that within a few years a "saturation" point is reached and the poisons spill out into the system .... find their way into the blood stream, and begin to look for tissue with which they have an "affinity". This, of course, is any weak or diseased part of your body .... There it deposits itself, and from this "beach head" spreads and destroys in all directions. Man calls this "end" result .... Cancer. In reality it is nothing more than the operation of a Law of Nature which says, ALL THAT IS WEAK MUST PERISH. Cancer is Nature's coup d'etat. Her final edict that she is "done with you". You have repeatedly ignored her warnings .... (no one suddenly "gets" a degenerative disease), and that now the balance of your body has been upset to the point of no return.

The same action occurs within the body of a cancer victim as occurs when a scientist "Kills" a mineral or plant; with his chemicals:

The elements which compose the substance fly apart and seek a new affinity. For remember,

Liberation

NOTHING DIES. Heated, chemicalized food is for this dead and dying (changing) age. It is for the diseased, decaying bodies of your predecessors. Do not YOU as aware Aquarian Children make the same "mistakes" (later you will see that there are no "mistakes"... all is happening according to divine Plan) as your Parents of the flesh.

On the subject of meat and fish little need be said. Even those who are far removed from the Spiritual Path are becoming vegetarian today, because all are cognizant of the harmful side effects of meat eating. But even if our meat were free of the cancer causing synthetic female hormones, the cancer disease causing antibiotics, even the disease cancer itself, it still would not be fit food for humans.

Man's whole physiological nature is herbivorous.... from his teeth to his intestine. Under certain geographical circumstances he must eat meat to survive, but a close look will reveal that the Karma involved in that situation is very "heavy". For you who have evolved Spiritually to the point to be living where there

Liberation

are Vegetables, fruits, nuts, grains, seeds, milk and milk products, unfertile eggs, (yolk only), there is no necessity to kill another sentient thing for your survival. More on this when we get into the Fourth commandment.

Many vegetarians do not eat dairy products or unfertile eggs. They are denying their bodies a source of nutrition that is unsurpassed in any other food. The keen observer can generally tell the difference between the Vegetarian and the Lacto-Vegetarian and this difference becomes more pronounced with the passing years. Man should be strong, and radiate vitality and Health, anything less is a denial of his birthright. There is beauty and inspiration in the words: "I do not eat anything that runs away from me". The plants too have a consciousness, but in Nature's scheme of things, they are grateful to be of use to a higher consciousness at the completion of their Life Cycle. The progression of the life force can be seen in the Plant sustaining itself from the mineral life, the animals sustaining themselves from the plant life, and Man sustaining himself,

Liberation
in the best possible way, from the products of Animals. Some today have been influenced by early nutritional authorities who have convinced them that Animal products are "mucous forming". This is true if the milk, cheese or eggs are pasteurized or cooked, just as all foods are "mucous forming" that have been heated. Milk, cheese and eggs are no more mucous forming than any other cooked food, besides which, the body needs a certain amount of mucous to gather up and expel harmful bacteria. So do not become fanatic on the subject of nutrition. Food Laws are simple and basic: Eat everything raw. Do not eat anything that has been changed or altered from its original structure, and eat nothing that has had any chemical added to it. The Father has provided you with the High Protein foods all the year round. By the eating of milk, cheese and egg yolks (avoid the white), you will nourish yourself so easily and well, that very little time and energy need be spent on the thought of food . . . . you will find that the vegetarian's time and thought is largely taken

Liberation

up with the demands of his ill-nourished body .... the end result of this is fanaticism.

In addition to the above suggestions, there are a few other thoughts you should keep in mind concerning nutrition: Eat only when you feel the call of hunger, and do not confuse "appetite" with hunger. Hunger is unmistakable. It is a slight (at first) pleasant "pain" in the stomach. Wait for this "call" before responding with what it should have ... (not what it "wants"). The stomach is like a slave ... It must take what you give it .... But mistreat it, and when you are least expecting it, it will revolt and "do you in". The man of The Spirit eats first and last for NUTRITION. Before eating anything, ask yourself, "Is this what my body needs? (Start thinking of your body as separate and apart from YOU). How well will this nourish my vehicle?"

Do not drink any liquid with your meals (milk is alright, for it "curds" when it enters the stomach and becomes a solid). Any liquid will interfere with the digestive process for it will dilute the digestive juices and make them less

Liberation

effective. Chew every bit of food thoroughly, until it becomes a liquid paste in the mouth before swallowing. The thorough mixing of food with the saliva is vital to the first step of digestion. If ALL would just eat, and observe this simple rule, they could live easily on half the amount of food usually eaten, thus alleviating the world's food situation overnight, as well as nourishing themselves much better. As was said, you may drink milk with your meals but it is of great importance that you "chew" each mouthful before swallowing. Include One or More of the Protein foods with each meal. Don't make the mistake that most vegetarians make, in not getting enough protein. These vegetarians stand out like dying flowers in a vase. Your body must be STRONG to withstand the POWER OF THE LIGHT, otherwise you will receive only as much as you can bear, the same as the current of electricity that is able to run the most delicate machinery, or manifest a light in the incandescent lamp. Give the LIGHT an organ or machinery or "low" or "high" form and it

Liberation
will manifest according to the capacity of the entity. Its manifestations may be "low" or "clumsy", or "high" and perfect . . . . it all depends upon the "material through which it functions. There is but ONE LIFE FORCE operating through ALL LIFE, but the DEGREE with which IT flows is dependent upon the STRENGTH OF THE ORGANISM. Make this realization your own.

Obtain a Grain and Nut grinder, and avoid any and all seeds or nuts that have been cracked, pealed or otherwise tortured, as they are rancid, and it is agreed today that the quickest way of making yourself sick with one of the degenerative diseases is by the taking into the body of . . . . rancid oils! Avoid all commercial bread . . . even the "whole wheat". If you must have bread eat only that which is ground (grains are as perishable as milk) first day fresh, and baked that day, and eaten that night. Avoid this "staff of Life" entirely unless it meets these qualifications.

. . . "or knife" . . . . The cruelest, most inhuman error, possible to make with a baby

Liberation

boy, is circumcision. The harm done to the delicate psyche of the new baby during this senseless operation cannot be exaggerated. The claim of cleanliness is absurd, for it is no more difficult to wash the penis during a bath than any other part of the body. Then why the need for this archaic ceremony? Circumcision has been part of the cultural ritual among certain peoples from ancient times, and as such it has served two functions: Tribal identification, and a painful test, at puberty, of manhood. Among most societies of this Planet it was not practiced until the advent of modern medicine with its fetish for sterile cleanliness. Cleanliness at any cost . . . and the cost has been greater than any have imagined, manifesting in insecure, timid children, the karmic spawn of ignorance and narrow mindedness. Every opening to the body has its natural protection. The eyes: the lids; The nose: millions of hairs; The mouth: the lips; The ears: the intricate canal; the anus: the two large gluteus maximus muscles: The vagina: the lips; the penis: the foreskin. When in his arrogance MAN picks up his scalpel to

Liberation

mutilate a divine body, what he is doing actually is saying to the Creator, "alright God, you have done a pretty good job in the designing of this body but you "goofed" here, but don't let that bother you, I'll take care of your mistake"!

When ANY Organ is removed or cut from the body, the whole functioning process of the body is hampered . . . . It means that the other sympathetic Organs must take up the added burden of the non-functioning, mutilated, or missing entirely . . . member. The additional burden placed upon the already weak (for no single part of the body is "sick" by itself), overworked parts of the body result in an early malfunction and poor performance . . . . with the ensuing ill health and premature death. Many are the lives that could have been "saved" after becoming aware, if it had not been that certain vital organs had been removed through surgery, prior to the knowing that "another way" was possible. But so much for this . . . . we are concerned here with prevention . . . . not cures. Sleep is our final consideration

Liberation
of the Third Commandment and fittingly brings us to the end of our discussion.

To understand the how and why of sleep, you should become aware of the cycles of Universal Life energy. At dusk, the world (your part of the world), goes into its lowest ebb, reaching the point of what could be called complete rest around 9:00 p.m. This relaxing of "Forces" continues until a little past midnight when imperceptibly the ascending currents of Life Energy begin to unfold and give birth to a new day, reaching its full momentum around the hour of 4:00 a.m. The best possible time for sleep then is between the hours of 9:00 p.m. and 4:00 a.m. with the heaviest sleep before midnight. Haven't you ever noticed during those times that you were out late, and were very tired, you seemed to get new life and energy after 1:00 a.m.? The tiredness left the body to be replaced with new vitality which easily kept you going the rest of the night. At that time you were experiencing this Natural Law. Should you continue to violate this rhythm of the Universe, the end penalty would

Liberation

be what the psychologists are fond of calling a psychosis. No Natural Law can be broken with impunity. Man-made laws can be broken without penalty, if you are not "caught", but the Laws of God are impossible to evade.

ALL are subject. All who transgress must pay. As we read in the "Dead Sea Scrolls".... "Disease is punishment by Nature for disobedience to her Laws". And that, my little ones, is "right on". I well realize that the obeying of the Third Commandment will mean a complete and radical change in some of your lives. Now is the time for courage of conviction. If you feel that the above is "truth" then use that wonderful God given gift of Will Power, and decide to LIVE the Third Commandment for 30 days. If you succeed, a new habit pattern will be formed and you will have taken the first step upon the ladder of Liberation. Perseverance furthers, (remember?). It is only difficult in the beginning. When you begin to experience the "rewards" no amount of temptation could convince you to return to your

Liberation

old habits of living. Be of strong heart.

Remember . . . . . . YOU ARE NOT ALONE.

*"Allow each vibration to complete
its own cycle, without interference"*

Of all the Commandments, this is the most beautiful and profound. Within these few simple Aquarian words lie most of the "Thou Shalt Nots" of the past ages. Read it again and "feel" the cognition of it. These are not the words of a "vengeful, wrathful God", but rather the admonition of a gentle, sweet, loving Father speaking to his Spiritually aware Son.

We all know today that nothing is "solid" that all is in constant change, and motion. All is "vibration" traveling at different rates of speed which we perceive through one or more of our five senses. What you may not know is that ALL is ALIVE. Science speaks of "creating Life", as if there were anything "dead in the Universe! Science may change one life form into another, but to Create life from a "dead" substance is not possible for there is nothing dead. If one thing were to be without Life, the whole Universe would crumble, and dissolve,

Liberation

for ALL is interdependent . . . . . . and that would mean that there was something else besides the Creation. All must be from the one Life . . . . And all that is from the One Life is Alive. there is no dead substance in the Universe....There can be none . . . For LIFE CANNOT DIE . . . . . ALL IS ALIVE . . . . . AND LIFE IS IN ALL.

ALL are interdependent. When something appears to die, yes, even your own body, what it does is merely change its form and structure. The elements which make up your vehicle, the Earth, Fire, air, Water and Ether composed of the electrons, atoms and molecules are no longer held together by the cohesive attraction of the Soul and so separate and form new affinities in keeping with the Law that all vibration will desert its present position for a higher position upon the first opportunity. Science has seen this fickleness in the atom and marveled at how the Atom will desert its mate for another of a higher vibration, should the opportunity present itself.

Liberation

This is in keeping with the Law of Evolution, which says, ALL VIBRATION MUST EVER CONTINUE TO RISE UPWARD ON THE SCALE OF ETERNAL HARMONY.

The Obeying of this Fourth Commandment will save man untold suffering and misery, for the "karma" is very heavy for those who break this Commandment. The effects from the causes set in motion due to the ignorance of this LAW can be seen everywhere today . . . . . The ecology problem, wars, intolerance, sickness, disease and death. The Karma for the disobedience to this commandment extends from the killing of a man, to the picking of a flower, and until this Law is experienced in your consciousness there can be little communication on the mental level. This Law must be "felt" . . . . up until now you have been living by your five senses, and you are just beginning to develop a "sixth sense," an intuitive sense. Many of you have had "flashes" where words were not necessary. You KNEW what was being thought, You FELT the vibration present without thought. At

Liberation

this time you were experiencing your sixth sense. This observation can only be lived within . . . . it cannot be explained.

The discovery of your intuitive sense is one of the most satisfying joyful experiences which awaits you, and is well worth any effort to develop. Those who live in their sixth sense have become One with the Father. It is the Nirvana of the Hindu, the Heaven of the Christians, and the bliss of the Moslems while living. You do not have to "die" to have the experience, it is yours now . . . . . But, before you can take from anything, something must be put in . . . and this something is a reverence for ALL LIFE. From this will come "HARMLESSNESS". When this realization becomes part of you, you have secured the first rung of the eight step ladder to Liberation.

So do not take the Life of anything needlessly . . . . If it is necessary for your survival to take the life of a plant . . . . pick it when ripe, when its cycle is over. If you did not make use of it at this time, it would dissolve itself and begin the process over again in the hope of being able

Liberation
to "serve you" the next time around.

YOU are GOD to all the minerals, plants and animals. Science is discovering the "mind" quality within ALL Life today. Tomorrow, Science will discover the Love and adoration that all the "lower" forms of life have for MAN. But except for the rare few . . . . . this realization must wait for the Golden Age to have mass consciousness. YOU with your beautiful Soul are longing to KNOW . . . . . Desire is the "instrument of His Will" So you WILL know, and SOON, how important you are in God's plan. With the knowledge will come a peace and happiness that "passeth all understanding" for there is no better feeling in life than that of being "useful". "Not Killing" . . . extends to the destroying of thoughts, enthusiasm, ideas, or beliefs of another. It extends to all levels of consciousness. Who are you to say that another "should not be where he is"? Or, "should not think what he is thinking". ALL are progressing as they should according to their Karma, be it mineral, plant, animal or Human. If it so happens that you have

Liberation

something to give, never fear, your vibration will attract those who are ready to receive what you have to offer. You do not need to push your ideas, criticize another, find fault, slander, or evangelize. These negative actions are the part and parcel of the fanatic who has found a little truth, which he himself is unsure of, and so continually seeks substantiation; for his own limited faith and understanding. He feels that if he can convince you, then, after all, he must be right! Avoid such people, they are vexations to the Spirit. But do not find fault with them. They too serve a purpose. They too will some day "arrive" where you are, and if you are not careful they may surpass you on the way. For all are being pressured to return from whence we ALL came. To be negative to life then in any form, be it the life of a mineral, plant, animal, or thought, is destructive to your own self, for never forget this great occult truth: "Whenever you harm another . . . . you harm yourself". ONE is part of the ALL and ALL is in the ONE. Make this realization your own for it leads to Freedom.

*"Possess nothing that you do
not need, and share all that you have"*

It was not by chance that this, the Fifth Commandment occupies the place that it does. We are living in what is known in the occult as the fifth period of humanity's evolution. We are part of the "Fifth Root Race" expressed in the five races of man, his present five senses, the five known elements, etc. If there is any one general characteristic common among the Aquarian Children it is their lack of possessions, and their willingness to share what they have.

You are about to scale a great height, the lighter you can make yourself, the easier will be the climb. The past age labored under a system of "credit" which provided them with "things" that they were told they needed, and as a result they became so burdened down with debt and obligations that their perception became cloudy, their energy wasted. Finally, sick and disillusioned at heart, they retired in their misery to await the grave. Lives wasted,

Liberation

opportunity lost. Despair and bitterness prevail everywhere. Why? Because the "things" that they thought they needed became their Master and they the slave, and so it must always be . . .
. . WHATEVER IT IS THAT MAN DIRECTS HIS ATTENTION TO, HE WILL BECOME A PART OF THAT. Remember this, for it is another Great Principle of Truth.

The smallest effort on your part will provide you with all that you need for shelter, food and clothing, and if these necessities are kept to a minimum you will find yourself free to direct your time and energies into whatever channel you choose. In the past, upon realizing this, you retired to a Himalayan Cave, the Jungle, or desert, and lived a selfish life of devotion, and so you had to return in this Iron Age to work out your Karma . . . . . for all must work . . . . . Can we do any less than our Heavenly Father? Witness the forces of nature . . . all work, from the tiniest electron to the biggest star. How should you work, what you should do, will be revealed to you when you have learned "To

Liberation

listen to the voice of the soul, and seek the light of the Spirit". So do not worry, do not concern yourself, it will come, it will come by your just BEING.

So now, simplify your life. Have the courage to take a good hard look at everything you have thought that you needed. If anything you possess comes under the heading of "burden", or "excess", discard it. This does not mean "obligations". Obligations can be worked out of, but never discarded, if you try to avoid obligations, they will return to haunt you.

In the simplification of your life by eliminating unneeded "things" you will find that the less you have, the more easy it is to share what you have, and the more time, money and energy is available to help your less fortunate brothers. You are not, however, to "aid" anyone if it is to your own detriment. Your first duty is to take care of yourself. The possessions that you feel are necessary for that purpose can be of the highest quality. Beauty and quality are not incompatible with Spirituality. There is no necessity for you to

Liberation

live the life of an ascetic, BUT, if you are materially attached to any possession that is not a necessity, you may uncover the most insidious deterrent to achieving Liberation: Attachment to ANYTHING of the Earth.

*"The Man and his Woman are One,
let nothing separate them"*

The Sixth Commandment exemplifies the Sixth Root Race . . . . The time of the Gods. The Sixth day of creation spoken of allegorically in the bible as the Sixth day, when man was created in the "image" of God, and there was no difference between them. In this Age ALL will be seen in the One, and One in the ALL. Why then should there be a necessity for the present day practice of divorce, or the leaving of a "Mate"? After a Love selection is made, there cannot be an "acceptable" excuse for making a change on the Spiritual level. "Incompatibility" belongs to the dense material vibration you are leaving. What if our Heavenly Father were to cast you aside, should you perform in a manner "less" than what was expected of you? The question of forgiveness does not arise . . . . There is nothing to "forgive". When you understand ALL . . . . you can "forgive" ALL. Those who "judge", are "disappointed", "find fault", etc., have not yet

Liberation

seen the divine Plan behind everyone and everything.

Should you make the error of separating yourself from your chosen Mate for the "greater merits" of another, you will find to your regret that you have merely exchanged ten sets of faults for a different "ten sets of faults".

Most of the marital problems that existed in the Piscean Age were the result of Man not knowing who he was and where his duties lay. The "fault" must rest with the Man, for Man is responsible for his Woman. Just as the Moon revolves around, and is dependent upon, the Sun, the Woman's whole life revolves around, and is dependent upon, her Man. All but the most Spiritually blind have seen that this fifty-fifty proposition cannot work.

Man is governed by the same Laws that are in operation throughout Nature. These Laws are constant and unchanging. In every evolving entity there is a Natural chain of command and performance. This effects Man in this way: Man is responsible to God . . . . Woman is responsible to Her Man . . . . Their children are

Liberation

fed from the "plastic fantastic" pap bottles of a sick society, until what is abnormal, appears to you as "normal". Only the most evolved Souls will "feel" the truth of these words . . . . The others must sooner or later come to this realization. How much wiser it is to learn through a "teacher" and avoid the "experience" rather than having to go through, and learn from the experience itself. But either way you will learn this lesson. Love and Faith in the teacher is the easy way . . . . . Life teaches with a big stick! FAITH is only necessary to achieve any of the levels of consciousness at the beginning . . . . Later on your Faith is rewarded by certain knowing.

So men, unless you are psychologically and Spiritually ready to assume your rightful place as the "Head" of the family, you should question your motives for wanting a Mate. If these motives are founded solely upon a sexual need, it would be better in the long run, if you were honest enough to say to the image of your desire, "I lust you Baby", not, "I Love You". Don't confuse lust with Love. Those who

Liberation

fed from the "plastic fantastic" pap bottles of a sick society, until what is abnormal, appears to you as "normal". Only the most evolved Souls will "feel" the truth of these words . . . . The others must sooner or later come to this realization. How much wiser it is to learn through a "teacher" and avoid the "experience" rather than having to go through, and learn from the experience itself. But either way you will learn this lesson. Love and Faith in the teacher is the easy way . . . . . Life teaches with a big stick! FAITH is only necessary to achieve any of the levels of consciousness at the beginning . . . . Later on your Faith is rewarded by certain knowing.

So men, unless you are psychologically and Spiritually ready to assume your rightful place as the "Head" of the family, you should question your motives for wanting a Mate. If these motives are founded solely upon a sexual need, it would be better in the long run, if you were honest enough to say to the image of your desire, "I lust you Baby", not, "I Love You". Don't confuse lust with Love. Those who

Liberation

insist upon staying in the lust vibration will pay (are paying) a very "heavy" Karma today. But this is a subject for the Seventh Commandment and will be explored next. The role of the Man is the same as the role of the Sun to the Moon. <u>He protects and provides for His woman. He is the strength which gives her STABILITY. He shines His light upon Her, and She radiates Her beauty to ALL.</u> He holds Her close to him through His magnetic Power of Love and Attraction. He expects Her to go through "changes" brought about by external influences . . . . . But he remains Constant . . . . Strong . . . . Reliable. He is Her security . . . Her Life . . . . Her reason for BEING. If the Sun had the Moon do His job for him there would be confusion, and Death in the World. The Moon would be completely inadequate for the job. Just as a woman, who is sent by her man out into the world to "help meet the bills". From this confusion comes resentment. Very often "unconscious" resentment, manifesting itself in discontent, nervousness, and a vague feeling that ALL is "not right". She senses a

61

Liberation

"weakness" in her man and begins to "test" his strength by nagging, peevishness, and the giving of a general "hard time" to her mate. Woman must be held safe. First by the Father of the flesh, or a "substitute", next by Her Man . . . . . do not be misled by the apparent safety of all that concrete and steel . . . . It is still a jungle out there, and your Woman is ill equipped to cope with it. If you both live by the Fifth commandment, you will find there is little necessity to expose each other to "roles" that are contrary to your "instincts". All this places a heavy responsibility upon the man, but he is well equipped by Nature to handle it.

A woman's emotional and physical equipment was meant to be used in quite a different direction: Her instinct is to nest. She is the Mother of All Living. This does not mean just her own offspring. The perfect Woman is both Wife and Mother, to Her Man. In God's Great Plan hers is the most vital role . . . . . For She is the "Shakti Power", The Creative Force in the Universe. As such, HOWEVER SHE "SEES" HER MAN, THAT

Liberation

IS MOST LIKELY WHAT HE WILL BECOME. The DUTY, the Natural function of a Woman, is to inspire and Serve Her Man. This "inspiration" should not be along the lines of criticism or fault finding, ever. Your man must be "right" even when he's "wrong". If you feel He is making a mistake .... Let Him make it. All that He should ever "feel" from you is a confident expression of His ability and Power. This is not a lie .... for you did feel this initially in your relationship, otherwise you would not have accepted Him as your Mate. If anything has come up to change this original "feeling" then it's a matter of Karma for you, which you must "work out" and live through. So do not "question the decisions" of your Man. If He is "wrong" it is far better that He find this out for Himself, rather than have You "save" Him from the lesson.

After all .... What are these "big decisions" anyway? At Best they end with one lifetime only, and have only to do with the gross Material World. Your goal is Liberation, so do

Liberation

not allow yourself to get caught in these mundane machinations of living. A Great master once gave the secret that would settle every dispute if used judiciously by the Woman: "I am sorry", "You are right", and "It's the Will of God". No, my Loved Ones . . . neither role is an easy one at first. Both can expect "pain" from the attempt to rise to the high Vibration of the Sixth Commandment . . . . But, "all birth is preceded by pain". Later, the rewards are so satisfying that you would not exchange your role for anything!

"Squander not your Creative Force in lust, but come together only when the three vibrations of the physical, mental, and emotional are in harmony with Spiritual Love"

You who are called "Hippies" today (and that seems to be anyone with natural hair), are going to "blow" a few minds, and perhaps your own as well, when out of the "mud" you emerge as the most moral of human Beings, with the highest standards of behavior. The Evolutionary Force is insisting today with the strongest possible pressure, that Man free His Soul from the bindings of the five deadly passions that have ruled, and controlled Him throughout His past lifetimes. You All know what these impediments are, but let us review them here: They are; anger, lust, greed, attachment, pride. You can see that the Seventh Commandment does not just mean a sexual "coming together", but whenever you have contact with another BEING your physical, mental and emotional vibrations should be free of these outworn

Liberation

emotions. I say outworn, for there was a time when they were useful to you, and you, or your tribe, could not have survived without them . . . but that need is over . . . . now let them die a natural death. Do not blame yourself too much should they rear their ugly head from time to time, for they are still "a part of you" the only difference now is that YOU are in CONTROL OF THEM. They are no longer in control of you. But they all die a "hard" death, so be as patient with yourself as you would another. But for you who will finally master the Truths laid down in this book, there is no question of "effort". Your actions will always be in Harmony with Spiritual Love. You will live in your Higher Consciousness, and will be guided by your "Spiritual Sense". You will be the First Aquarians. Great will be your reward, in Earth and Life Hereafter!

At the time of sexual union, the strongest emotions that man and woman are capable of knowing are called into play, sending out their vibrations into the "Blue Ether" in search of a

Liberation

Soul that is vibrating on the same "frequency". If you should conceive a child with a vibration of lust and animal passion, this will be the Soul that left the body in his last life on Earth while immersed in the same vibration you are creating. Like attracts Like. Strike C sharp on a tuning fork, and if there is another C sharp in the vicinity, it will begin to vibrate, the Vibration set in motion having found an affinity. A tuning fork pitched to any other "note" will remain unaffected.

So . . . . Your combined CALL, will create a "groove" for your KARMIC Child to enter the dense Earth atmosphere upon. Much as a river cuts its path through the mud allowing the young springs to flow easily into it. This Soul, responding to your vibration, enters the ovum along with the sperm and begins to draw forth the materials for its earth expression from the mother by gestation. The type of body that it will form for itself is dependent upon its Karma. In this, the Cusp Period for the Age of Aquarius, a child conceived in lust will bring the heaviest kind of Karma upon the parents.

Liberation

Unless your baby is desired, with the knowledge that you are engaged for the main purpose of releasing a deserving soul, you will receive an offspring that will require a tremendous amount of work and effort to raise his vibration to that of the New Age requirements. It can be done, and many are doing it . . . . but at what a cost to nerves and peace of mind! These are the parents who will read these words and sadly nod their heads. Theirs is a great responsibility. If they accept the challenge and do their duty, great will be their reward, otherwise . . . . "heavy" their Karma. Those of you who will dedicate each union to god's evolutionary "plan" and join together with Love in your Heart and a peaceful compassionate Vibration, will send out a Harmonious pitch of such pure quality that will penetrate through the Blue Ether, into the Light, and there arouse a Soul from its rest who left the body a "Saint" in its last life, and will be a World Savior in this One. Such a Soul will give joy and happiness to its parents, and be a blessing to all who see him. You who can act

Liberation

selflessly in this "Iron Age" for the betterment of Humanity, will "feel" the whole Universe sing your praises.

Making Love is a joyful thing . . . . Making Love selflessly with a High purpose is God-Like. In Every living organism there is a Natural Cycle. If after a "period of adjustment" you can limit your sex acts to the Woman's natural Creative Cycle of once a month, you will build within yourselves a Great reservoir of Power and Strength which you can use for "creative purposes". How this comes about will be made clear to you later. One of the obvious "side effects" from the exercise of this control is that there is no way that you could ever grow "tired" of your Mate. The Great Saints and Sages from time immemorial practiced celibacy, for there is no better way to hasten Spiritual "progress" than by controlling the Creative Force within You, along with the other "Observances". Happily, it is not necessary to do without sex. But it is necessary to gain Mastery over this force and control it to do Your bidding, according to a regular Cycle,

Liberation

planned by Nature. The limiting of your desire will make you Master over the strongest creative Force know on the Earth Level, and you will be able to use this power positively in whatever direction you see fit. Your meditations, for example, will become so strong that the vibrations you send out will set into effect new causes which can change the very course of Humanity's destiny!

You have heard of the Holy men who are located in various parts of the World and by their positive Vibrations, they influence and work for the betterment of humanity, without moving from the area? Simply by creating harmonious, peaceful thought waves they do this. The "Pranas" instead of being eliminated through the lower levels of consciousness are raised, and used to stimulate the centers within the brain which bestow unlimited Power upon their Master. This is the power that will be yours when you have mastered your sex urge . . . the World needs you, my Loved Ones.

"Each morning join your vibration with the ascending currents of Universal Life Energy using the method your Earthly Spiritual Father has taught you"

With this, The Eighth Commandment, you will learn how to draw upon the never failing supply of Life Force, Wisdom, Strength and Power, which surrounds us, and within which we live, move and have our BEING. Within each of us is the same "SUBSTANCE" AS WITHOUT. The only thing that keeps us separate from ALL POWER is our own feeling of separateness. Right now You are like onto the little drop of water that is cast upon the sand. It has a limited life of separateness because it has been removed from the ocean . . . let the drop return to the ocean and once again it enjoys ALL POWER for it has the strength of the "PARENT" behind it. If you should analyze a drop from the ocean or a drop from a pond you will be able to ascertain ALL of the qualities of the BODY of water from which it sprang, for the drop is of the Ocean or Pond. Similarly, you have all of the QUALITIES OF

Liberation

GOD within you, but due to your own feeling of separateness there is a thin layer of "NEGATIVITY" which separates you from ALL POWER. Much as the thin skin that surrounds an air bubble. Within the air bubble and without, is the same. Burst the bubble and this "separation" ceases to exist. And this is exactly what you are going to learn how to do!

You are about to learn a great secret of the "Masters", one which was practiced during the days of Atlantis . . . . taken from there by a few of the survivors to the Middle East where the secret was practiced by the Ancient Alchemists, under the guise of seeking to find a way to turn the baser metals into gold. During this period of man's evolution, anyone caught doing, or saying, anything against, or different from, the prevailing opinion of the "priests" would have been tortured, and put to death. Then, as now, material wealth was the only respected power, and so these sages of the times gathered together as "scientists" working for the status quo. Their mysterious comings and goings and

Liberation

long periods spent in their underground "laboratories" (temples) with their minerals and chemicals, was looked upon with respect and anticipation by the powers of the moment, so that their real work, that of laying the foundation for the Age we are now leaving, was left unmolested. Some of you, reading this for the first time will feel a strange affinity for these great Souls. Perhaps you were there? Well, it doesn't matter . . . . . You are here now, and you can practice this exercise in the open without fear of persecution. The exercise of which I speak is the Pentagram Exercise . . . . Better known as the Star Exercise. "The Philosopher's Stone", "The giver of All Wisdom", the "Way to ALL Power", the "Elixir of Life", and many more wonderful titles. The Star Exercise cannot be exaggerated or praised too much. The Pentagram is the symbol of the Fifth Root Race. The sign of Humanity's Fifth period of evolution . . . . . It is NOW! You who knowingly practice this exercise in the morning before the dawn, when the channels are the clearest, will play the most vital role in the ushering in of the next

Liberation

age, which will be symbolized by the Six pointed Star .... The star of balance and wisdom. The Powers prevailing never ask of you anything, without rewarding your efforts. The immediate benefits to you will be one of increased confidence, courage, strength, power and wisdom. I know that it sounds too "way out" to be believed, so I do not ask anything more of you than that you will give the Star Exercise a thirty day "trial" period, and perform it in the prescribed manner without "cheating". Which means .... without missing a morning . . . or skipping any of the "steps". Then decide for yourself.

The most beautiful thing about the Star Exercise is that, even if the most skeptical will take the position of the five pointed Star, and perform the exercise in the following manner, he will notice an inflow of Universal Life Energy into his body. Those who have confidence and FAITH in it efficacy will, of course, receive much more from the exercise, due to their "clearer channels".

This is the way the Pentagram exercise is performed:

Liberation

In the morning an hour before the Dawn, take your bath and stand nude over the spot on which you will later meditate, and make of your body a five pointed Star by spreading your legs and extending your arms straight out from the shoulders to the side. Your left palm should be turned up, and the right palm turned down, your head erect. Your body should be alert, but relaxed. The first part of the exercise will stimulate, repair and improve the memory gland. Arch your body, stretch the arms back, throw your head back, concentrate your eyes at a point as high as you can (keeping them closed), and begin rapid breathing with a STEADY rhythm. This manner of breathing is called by the Yogis, "breath of fire". Count to yourself one hundred and eight times. Hold the last inhale as long as you comfortably can, and resume your original upright position on the exhale. Allow the arms to drop to the side and begin deep long breathing, just as deep and long as you can, keeping a steady rhythm. When you feel relaxed in the shoulders, raise the arms once more, and look at the left

Liberation

upturned palm, inhale and think, "I", turn and look at the right hand, exhale, and think, "AM". Now repeat this for from one to three minutes depending upon your stamina, then inhale, face front, with the eyes closed, and hold your breath comfortably, exhale easily, hold out and relax. Lower the arms, continue rhythmic deep, long breathing until all tension has left the shoulders. Now begin a steady rhythmic upward and downward movement of the arms, keeping the arms straight. Inhale deep up, and exhale down, along with the movement of the arms. Continue for One to Three minutes. Inhale . . . . come back to the original Star position. Hold, and now concentrate on the Universal Life energy flowing through every part of your body, but especially through the upturned left hand. Exhale, easily, hold the position . . . . . . forget your breath, keep the eyes focused at the "third eye position" inhale, HOLD and repeat this Affirmation to yourself: "I AM POSITIVE TO MIND, ENERGY AND MATTER AND CONTROL THEM ALL. I AM NEGATIVE ONLY TO THE ABSOLUTE

Liberation
WHICH IS THE CENTER OF BEING, OF WHICH I AM. AND AS I ASSERT MY MASTERY OVER MIND, ENERGY AND MATTER, AND EXERCISE MY WILL OVER THEM, SO DO I ACKNOWLEDGE MY SUBORDINATION TO THE ABSOLUTE, AND GLADLY OPEN MY SOUL TO THE INFLOW OF DIVINE WILL, STRENGTH, POWER AND WISDOM". Exhale. Hold the position until you must inhale, and then relax, sit down and begin your Meditation.

This is the most ancient Affirmation known to the "Masters" today, handed down from teachers who have received it from "higher" teachers and so on, and on, higher and higher, until we come to those wonderfully developed Souls who have visited the Earth from their higher planes of BEING, of which you will learn . . . . . are many.

The Vibrations contained within this Affirmation have resounded throughout the World since time immemorial. If you will but repeat this vibration aloud and verbally, all of the

Liberation

"like" vibrations will be "attracted" to YOUR Vibration, raising you higher .... higher .... and HIGHER. Always just as much as you can bear.

When you "get into" the Star exercise you will actually "feel" the "Pranas" being sucked into your body by the pumping action of your heart. The symbol of Love, common to all mankind. Slowly, but surely that thin film of negativity will be dissolved, opening yourself to the divine flow without. Much as a pin hole in a vacuumed container permits the outside "air" to rush in and fill the empty space.

You have heard the expression, "Nature abhors a vacuum". Now know the full meaning of this Law. Before the container can be filled, it must be empty. To be successful in opening the "doors" with the Spiritual Keys you are being given, you must empty yourself of your EGO, Your PREJUDICES, Your PRECONCEIVED IDEAS, in other words .... YOUR PERSONALITY which you have thought ... and still think ... is YOU. The time you recognize your ONENESS WITH ALL

Liberation

LIFE, that is the time when ALL LIFE WILL BOW DOWN AND SERVE YOU. All that you must do is open a crack in the shell you have covered yourself with as a defense "against" the "outside" world. Lifetime after lifetime has covered you with sheath after sheath to protect your Soul while it learned its lessons. All that you have done . . . . All that you have been . . . All that you now are, was to lead you to this moment!

The Star Exercise combined with Meditation and the chanting of The Great Affirmation (explained later) will burn away sheath after sheath, until finally you will experience a "rush" within. A current of Light and Sound fills every part of your BEING. There will be LIGHT without and LIGHT within . . . . Your WHOLE BEING will be immersed in the WHITE LIGHT OF GOD. The Divine Spark has returned to that from "whence it came". The CIRCLE has been completed in keeping with THE GREAT LAW OF VIBRATION. You, As a Divine Ray from the Sacred Fire will then emulate the Father. On the one hand You

Liberation

will receive All . . . . . with the other hand You will give . . . ALL.

You are needed now, more than at any other time of your past lifetimes. The seed is, "about to split the rock", and emerge into the LIGHT. You who will dedicate your lives to this effort will become immortal, the Saviors of all Mankind. Your prize will be "LIBERATION". Those who feel the effort too great will drift on to oblivion, tied to the Karmic Wheel of suffering, until once more, this same age rolls around, carrying with it the VIBRATION which their Soul has reached in its evolutionary development, and so will be able to relate to . . . and once more, they will be given this opportunity to work out their Karma and achieve LIBERATION while living. Your will is free . . . . . "Desire is the instrument of His Will" . . . . The choice is yours.

"Do every act energetically, intelligently, truthfully, and lovingly"

With the understanding and obeying of this Ninth Commandment, the Cycle of your Vibration completes itself, the ends of the circle curve around and join. Perfection is achieved, you have made of yourself a Sphere . . . . The perfect shape wherein the Center of your "I AM" is in balance with your circumference. This achievement will insure your place on the next plane, for it is in keeping with Nature's scheme of things. All manifestations have as their basis the same pattern, expressed through millions of ways . . . . . . And yet ONE: A SPHERE. This LAW may be seen in the electron, vapors, raindrops, mercury, red and white blood corpuscles, and on and on to the biggest Star. Even from there the Law keeps manifesting . . . . Our whole Universe is traveling through space at a tremendous rate of speed and is revolving around Itself, which in turn is revolving around a Central Sun, which is so far distant that our telescopes can not see

Liberation

it . . . . but astronomers know it is there. If our Universe could be viewed from that Sun . . . . . It would appear as a SOLID SPHERE! Fix this Law Of the Circle firmly in your mind, for from this wisdom will come an appreciation of the Oneness of ALL, and a release from the pettiness of Earthly matters.

Long before the Egyptian Pharaohs decided to use the Pyramids as "ego trips" for their Souls, these ancient Temples of the Masters were erected to serve as a guide to Liberation to all those who could "read" their secret. They serve as the perfect example of the Law of Cause and Effect, but even today, most still do not understand, for they see only the obvious. Their vision is in part, for the "truth" which they have is in part. None are ready for the Truth unless their Soul has earned the "right" to hear it from their past Karma. Knowing this, there is "no blame". There is no "disappointment". The Master expects no "results". He and his Truth ARE. It is here for ALL now. It has always been available, but one can only see, what one is ready to "see".

Liberation

For you who are ready now, this is the Secret of the Pyramids: The ponderous base represents the low dense vibration of the Planet Earth, the corners represent the means of transcending this vibration. The peak represents ultimate achievement . . . . Liberation. Looking down from the top, we can see the even stratum on all four sides which enabled the pinnacle to be reached. The balance is perfect, so the center is perfect. If one of the sides were either less or more than it should be the center would be off, and perfection lost.

Men have stood for countless ages and gazed with awe-struck wonder at the grandeur of the Pyramid and pondered upon the significance of such a mighty monument. Allegorically, some have intuitively felt that the peak meant the ultimate religion, and so they stood at the base and attempted to scale the steep sides by the path of their choice. They disagreed among each other as to which was the best path, and so each group with its own leaders set out to climb by a different route. ALL went well until they neared the top, then they began to collide with

Liberation

each other, and so the great conflict of religions began, with the terrible cost of which you are all familiar. All the while the Great Pyramid somberly awaited the moment of disgust, and revulsion for what the brothers had done to each other to dawn upon them. It has taken thousands of years, but at last the light is dawning.

All religions lead to god, but ALL religions must bow reverently at the peak, and dissolve themselves into the ONE. Those who in combination made the religion, must SINGLY and alone . . . . travel the rest of the way. So now from this great, frightening height man must look down and see the four corners of the pyramid and know that they stand for: LIFE . . . MIND . . . . TRUTH . . . . LOVE . . . . To maintain his precarious footing, to sustain his present position achieved through countless lifetimes, Man must now work to extend the Stratum of the four corners of his OWN SQUARE evenly to join each other in perfect balance in order to reach SPIRIT, represented by the Peak of the Pyramid.

Liberation

Many on the Path today have seen "flashes" of Spirit through the use of psychedelic drugs, some of the minds were ill prepared for the experience and so were blown out by the power of the Light. Just as a fuse blows that is suddenly given too many amps. Other, more Karmically fortunate ones, were prepared for the experience, and went through a great metamorphosis which changed their lives. The wise ones have said, "once is enough there is no need to repeat the experience". For any chemical substance concocted by man will eventually prove destructive to the organism. LSD was meant for some of you to glimpse the great possibilities awaiting you, not to "hook you" on the experience. The psychedelic Drugs have served their purpose, (nothing "happens"), now you are ready for the High without a down, Whenever you perform an action ENERGETICALLY . . . . . INTELLIGENTLY . . . . TRUTHFULLY . . . . LOVINGLY, you Automatically build your vibration evenly, symmetrically, and balanced to the four square of your pyramid. Each time you perform an

Liberation

action which achieves this balance you raise your soul that much closer to the peak of Spirit. In fact you can forget about Spirit, and the Great Law of Cause and Effect will work for you, automatically raising yourself after each success! Finally your goal of Liberation is reached. There is no question of "failure". Be as one who fears no failure . . . . he courts no success . . . . just BE.

> *"When you have mastered these Commandments, leave the house of your Earthly Spiritual Father, and do the work of your Heavenly Father"*

With this, the Last commandment, the circle begins once more, only now on a "higher" plane. The Tenth commandment leads you to the first Level of consciousness of your new life on the highest plane possible, and still be of the Earth. The First commandment admonished you to "Obey and Live by the Teachings of your Earthly Spiritual Father", now you are to "Obey your Heavenly Father" as Masters of the Earth and all of its elements. You are the "Center" of your "Circumference", "Positive" to all you survey. You are "negative" only to the Absolute, who directs you in all that you do. Before performing any action, you have but to "tune in" to the Divine within and put yourself, as one Master said it, "on automatic pilot". The Positive current within will pull you through safe and unharmed. All illusion of separateness has gone. The "drop" has returned to the Ocean, and so once more has all the Power, and

Liberation
Strength of that from whence it came.

You and the Path have merged into One. You are no longer the "seeker" begging for the spiritual crumbs from the table of knowledge, but are a Master demanding (in the name of God) to have happen whatever it is you desire. And as long as you demand for "positive" reasons, you will be held safe in the bosom of the father, but should you use the Forces for your own selfish purposes, you will doom yourself to be destroyed by the very Forces you would have obey you. The forces obey the Black as well as the White Magician. The Black Magician believes that "Might makes right". The White Magician believes that "Right makes might". Knowing this simple "rule of thumb" You can easily "spot" which is which. The Forces may be used by anyone who has learned their secrets, but the penalty for misusing them is far too heavy a price to pay except by the most depraved of Souls.

Liberation

Beware of a sense of Pride in your great accomplishment. Stand humble in the knowledge that ALL WILL, AND INDEED MUST, arrive at the great height that you have achieved. Your experience is not unique. All of the great Saints and sages who preceded you share an equal part in your victory . . . . . for your accomplishment was also theirs . . . . Just as those who follow you will "owe" their success to the work which you will do. ALL IS INTERDEPENDENT . . . . ALL IS ONE.

Be prepared for "The Great Woe", for almost none will "see" you. Almost none will "hear" you. You will have to have the fortitude to watch those . . . . Yea, even those who are nearest to you, being sucked into the vortex of the grinding wheels of time. You must stand and hear their cries of anguish and despair . . . . helpless to aid. For unless they "see" you, you are powerless. Know at this time my Loved Ones, that All is well, and that the Father is doing the very best He can, and in the end will so appear.

Beware of falling into the last trap of the Holy

Liberation

man: Spiritual Ego! It matters little whether you have one follower or one million. That One may become a Spiritual Giant who will shake the very World from its lethargy, and the "million" may fade away into oblivion when you are no longer available to succor them. You are not to judge what the fruits of your actions should be. You are to do the work of the Heavenly Father with no thought of attachment to the end results. Any attachment on your part at this time will have the effect of removing your power, for attachment would mean that you have slipped back into the rut of thinking that YOU are doing it. Always remember, that You are nothing more than a servant of God. A good servant does not ask why. Does not question the Will of the Master, and is unattached to the results of his actions, for he does only what he is told to do, confident, that if he performs to the best of his ability, his Master will always take care of him regardless of what "appear" at the moment to be the results of his actions. The work in which you should be engaged will come to you, do not

Liberation

be anxious, or feel that there "must be more" you can do. DO THE WORK THAT IS IN FRONT OF YOU, obeying the Ninth commandment and you will discover that ALL work is important work. That there is no "high" or "low" work to do. Just as every note in a musical score has its place, and all the sounds are interdependent upon each other for harmony. Labor performed with Life, Mind, Truth, Love brings harmony to the Universe. leave out One part . . . . . and there is discord. Seek no further my Love, "for that which can never reach you from the outside" Listen for, and obey, "the voice of the Soul" You now walk in the "Light of the spirit" YOU ARE HIS SOUL . . . . . HIS SOUL AND YOU ARE ONE.

THE GREAT AFFIRMATION

"ONE GOD . . . . . .
    CREATES, CONSTITUTES,
    GOVERNS, SUSTAINS, AND
    CONTAINS, ALL . . . .
HIS NAME IS . . . .
    LIFE, MIND, TRUTH, LOVE, AND
    SPIRIT.
I AM HIS SOUL . . . .
    HIS SOUL AND I ARE ONE"

"THE GREAT AFFIRMATION"

The "mantra" for the New Age differs from all the other "chants" of the past Ages. Contained within these twenty-six Vibrations (two and six are eight . . . the number of perfection) are All the Love, and ALL the Wisdom of the New Age. From this awareness shall come the "balance" represented in the Six Pointed Star . . . the symbol of the Golden Age . . . . Better known as the Age of Aquarius

The chanting of this Affirmation will unite the Son with the Father. When the Son shall "see" the Father, he will love Him. Not because he was "told" to love Him, but because he now "knows" Him and so cannot help but Love Him! The Great Affirmation is not to be chanted without thought to the meaning of the words. Such an effort would be largely a waste of time and energy. At present the Spiritual atmosphere is "charged" with the "thought dust" of repetitious words thrown out as so much worthless sound of little value, by those who chant with limited understanding of what it

Liberation

is they are chanting. The "fault" is not entirely theirs however, for it is very difficult to think of the meaning of the words you are Vibrating while chanting in a foreign language!

The next great Spiritual awakening will come from the West, according to Ancient prediction. The Center of the circumference of THIS VIBRATION is Los Angeles . . . . The City of The Angels. (Don't laugh . . . . remember the Lotus grows in the mud) Spiritual Teachers from all over the World are being drawn to this city . . . . . . much as a light bulb draws into itself the greatest light . . . . before it goes out. But go out it, and they, must. They were "right" for the past and still are right for some, but a NEW VIBRATION is being born from the Old . . . . . To continue spreading the messages of yesterday's Spiritual influence . . . would be like carrying coals to Newcastle.

The First language of The World today is English. The Great Affirmation should be then, by simple reasoning . . . . . in English. The English language is the highest communication Vibration on the Planet Earth at the present time. The Vibration contained within this chant

Liberation

will Spread the fastest "circles". Can anyone not see this? All that is needed now are strong sons, who will be the future Earthly Spiritual Fathers to break with (not put down) tradition, and use the Old as the "substance" upon which to stand in order to reach the next step on the Evolutionary ladder.

Try chanting The Great Affirmation using your "intuitive sense" as to "method" and feel for yourself the Power contained therein. Never be afraid to "test your answers". Even your fondest beliefs and opinions should be able to stand the test of close scrutiny. If you are afraid to do this, then you will be held fast by the Vibration you are in, for you have applied the "brakes" to your own Spiritual evolution. The Affirmation does away with the "I am God" belief, which is an error born of the limited understanding of partial truth. This false teaching has taken possession of many of the Hindu "Masters" with the result that all is

Liberation

taught to be "Maya" or the "Great Illusion". This belief in the non-existence of matter has reduced millions of people to a passive negative state of mind which is now hindering the upward progress of Humanity. Those who hold the I Am God belief, are easily distinguished by their negative mental condition . . . . a natural result of absorbing the "nothingness" gospel of Maya. You are a Child of the Absolute and possessed of the Divine Heritage. Your whole purpose for being here is to unfold qualities which are LIKE the Heavenly Father. Do not make the mistake, as so many have done in the past, of confounding the Relative with the Absolute. With each new level of consciousness on the "seven" planes of existence you will take on a new and more splendorous body, and your powers will increase to the point where, to any and all on the lower planes, you would appear as God Himself, but there is but "ONE GOD" and ALL are subordinate to Him.

All the different manifestations of the Absolute are MENTAL CREATIONS of the

Liberation

Absolute . . . thought forms held in the Infinite Mind . . . The Infinite Spirit in them . . . They in the Infinite Spirit. ALL matter has no existence outside the "MIND" of the absolute, but that does not make it any the less "real". For the Real thing about the ALL is the SPIRIT involved in the THOUGHT FORM. The SPIRIT in the Soul of Man is the "SOUL OF THE SOUL" which is never born, never changes, and never ceases to be. This is the REAL self of Man in which indeed, He is ONE WITH THE FATHER. When man enters into the State of Conscious Unity with the ONE, he becomes more than Man . . . . More than the gods . . . . he is then, "in the bosom of the Father".

The First Vibration of The Great Affirmation is "ONE". ALL IS IN THE ONE, AND ONE IS IN THE ALL. There is nothing "outside" itself. God . . . . Allah . . . . Ram . . . . Brahma . . . . Jehovah. These are some of the names of the Absolute. They all have one thing in common . . . . . That is the AH sound. Is not this sound Universal and common to all men?

Liberation

It is the sound of adoration and Love. If you will hold the vibration "AH" within the Name of God, and project love and longing with your very last breath, your Vibration will carry through to the very ends of the Earth gathering, as it goes, all of the "thought dust" of lesser projections of the same sound made by those who spoke the Word with little or no thought to its power. This vibration can be likened unto a powerful magnet circulating in a barrel of nails. "Like attracts Like". The vibration coming from you must return to you when its projected force is spent. The "circle" completes itself over your own head, showering down its blessings upon you. Each thought form, each spoken word knows unerringly its own generator, and MUST, in keeping with the Great Law of the circle . . . . . Return to that, "from whence it came". Knowing this law, You can clearly see how important it is that your "projections" are Positive. For the "returned" Vibration works according to LAW, and returns in sometimes unrecognizable proportions in the form of "blessings" or

Liberation

"curses" . . . . ("As Ye Sow So Shall Ye Reap") depending, of course upon what YOU have created originally. Knowledge of the workings of this Law can change the very course of your destiny. Chanting the name of God, and allowing the Vibration to rise naturally to the highest pitch (note) you are capable of reaching, will stimulate the pituitary and pineal bodies of the brain, causing them to become active and to unfold your latent Powers.

The Pituitary and Pineal glands in Man's brain are at present dormant . . . . awaiting that time in Man's evolution when he will have arrived at the point of Awareness which will enable them to secrete . . . . At that time, Man will have the extraordinary Power of being able to see, "Past, present and future". As everyone knows, Man at present uses about one tenth of his brain capacity. Knowing what you do now about evolution, you can readily see that the "unused" portion of Man's brain is for use at a later date. But, as always, there are a few Great Souls who "point the way" to those who follow.

Liberation

They are always in advance of the rest of Humanity, and again, as always, humanity cannot see them, and even resents their presence . . . the herd's behavior is like the captive carnivorous animals who would tear the arm off the man who feeds them at the very first opportunity. "They" will accept "spirituality" as long as it is in a "palatable" form, and not too demanding. One trip a week for about an hour, to the "temple" is, "just about right". Some will read this and not appreciate the simple truths contained herein . . . . . others will have the dawning realization that Great Truths are always, "simple", and that if a thing is complicated or difficult to understand, it simply means that the writers or speakers themselves did not understand it. God himself is governed by the same Laws He has Created, so, from the finite Vibration of the relative, we pass on to the Infinite Vibration of the Absolute, and find that ALL emanates from the ONE and ALL must sooner or later return to the ONE. In Keeping with the Great Law of the Circle, "As above . . . so below", God is the Father-Mother of ALL MANIFESTATIONS,

Liberation

each entity a separate Vibration, a Creation of the First Cause. There are no two fingerprints in the World alike . . . . . There are no two Vibrations in the World alike.

You who have been filled with a sense of "smallness and "unreality" KNOW THAT YOUR REALITY IS SECOND ONLY TO HIS OWN. By Your Vibration He holds you SAFE. Just as the Earth Father "identifies" his child by sight . . . . . You are Identified by the heavenly Father by VIBRATION. You who can grasp this will be free forever from fear. You will have the comfort and satisfaction of KNOWING that you are held FIRMLY IN THE MIND OF THE INFINITE BEING . . . to such comes the knowledge that in LIFE THERE CAN BE NO DEATH. Each Vibration is KNOWN by the Father, and must return to "whence it came" Just as the thought Vibrations You give birth to must return to You! The only difference is that YOUR VIBRATION EMANATES FROM A FINITE

Liberation

MIND, AND SO HAS LIMITED LIFE; whereas the Thought forms of the Absolute emanate from an INFINITE MIND and so have EVERLASTING LIFE.

As an example which further explains the phenomenon, take the characters of the writers of fiction. They seem very real to us, and we weep, become angry, rejoice or feel sad as we follow them through their adventures, and yet they have no existence outside of the minds they are in at the moment. You can "give birth" to a whole army of people and watch them go through their different "numbers" and yet . . . . they have no existence outside your finite mind. Are you beginning to "see" just Who You are now? How trivial and unimportant seem all your trials and tribulations in the light of your new Wisdom! That which is REALLY YOU cannot be harmed, for IT IS HELD SAFE IN THE "MIND" of the father. All of your "problems" are the result of this sense of separateness which has been your mistaken belief throughout your countless past lifetimes . . . . . Truly now . . . . . have you not

Liberation

suffered enough?

. . . . CREATES . . . . The first activity of Any Creator, "below" or "above" is to Create. The Artist his painting, the Musician his music, the Philosopher his logic, the Mathematician his numbers, The absolute His Universe. Because everything is an emanation of the Absolute there can be nothing "Dead" anywhere. If anything is non-living, then the essence of God cannot be in it. Life is present in every form from the hardest mineral to the ether. ALL chemicals are alive, and from the earth, to man's body, there is but a continuous change of shape in form. When ANYTHING "dies" the atoms and other principles of which that entity is composed remain fully ALIVE AND ACTIVE. When the Soul leaves the body, the body is just as much "alive" as before, but now, because it has lost its "cohesive entity" (Soul) the electrons, atoms and molecules continue their activity, only now it is along the lines of dissolution rather than construction. But this "breaking" apart is only a temporary condition, for as these elements separate they immediately seek affinities they can relate to. Their next

Liberation

"form" may be a blade of grass in Rome, or your dining room table. THAT with which YOUR vehicle was formed was merely "borrowed" from the infinite supply of Universal Substance in order to form the Body which would best "express" the activity of your Soul in this present state of Evolution.

ALL BODIES ARE CREATED IN THE SAME WAY, be it a stone, flower or Human. An aggregate of Electrons makes the Atom. An aggregate of Atoms makes the Molecule . . . . The Molecule makes the Body. ALL brought together by the Great Law of Attraction . . . . . Better known as LOVE. Love indeed, "makes the world go round".

So, if the combination of Electrons, Atoms and Molecules are destroyed by chemical action, through the "death" of a body, the components then separate and LIVE THEIR SEPARATE LIVES until they come in contact with other similar "particles" with which they have an affinity, and a new Union is formed. Each dissolution of "form" finds the atoms ambitiously searching for ANOTHER FORM

Liberation

THAN ITS PRESENT, SEPARATE, STATE OF BEING WITH WHICH IT CAN RELATE! ALL in keeping with the Great Law of Evolution which says, "ALL VIBRATION MUST EVER CONTINUE TO RISE UPWARD ON THE SCALE OF ETERNAL HARMONY". So you see that "death" is an illusion. Our Creator has Created ONE LIFE, manifesting itself in countless forms and shapes. underneath ALL is the SPIRIT of Life pressing forward for expression, ALL is filled with Living Force, Power, Action, thrilling with Vitality, throbbing with feeling, filled with Activity. All is from the ONE LIFE and ALL is ALIVE! Death is the "Great Illusion". Death is the "Maya" . . . . NOT THE CREATION.

Creation does not necessarily mean "order", it could manifest in chaos (like an "abstract" painting) if the Creator did not next . . . . CONSTITUTE. This means that everything Created follows its own Evolutionary "path". This can be seen in the electron on a small scale, and the Planets on a large scale.

Liberation

Both are constituted the same, with their rotating and propulsory movements. Both are held within "their own orbit" by The Great Law working through CONSTITUTION, working simultaneously and Harmoniously with the Law of Love. To Each Creation is assigned a place and function, bringing ORDER to the universe, with the aid of God's Government. All is CONSTITUTED by exact Laws . . . . . five must always be "five". It can never be six, or lapse into "four". The Souls occupying temporarily their present vehicles are in a continual state of Evolution . . . . be it the "soul" of a rock or human. Their progression is GOVERNED by unchanging Laws, and no "step" on the Evolutionary ladder may be "skipped". This is why the "awareness" brought by the Psychedelics is temporary. five in attempting to be "Six" may get a glimpse of six, but the fall from that Great height could destroy the Mind . . . . leaving the Soul a helpless prisoner until once more a "Vehicle" is provided for its "potential" Liberation.

Open your eyes now my Loved Ones, and

Liberation

look around at the Janis Joplins, the Jimi Hendrixes, and the hundreds of other "unknown" children who have left the body to serve as examples for you to learn from. You are in the University called Earth, learn your lessons now and "pass" onto the next grade, or return to take the "class" over again. The choice is yours.

Finally the Creator CONTAINS ALL WITHIN himself. The Creation is not God, as some teach, but it is God who holds all secure within His Creation, much as a mother bird enfolds her young within her wings, protected . . . . . secure. There is Nothing "outside" Itself. ALL is CONTAINED WITHIN ITSELF.

"HIS NAME" . . . . Expresses itself in His manifestations of Life, Mind, Truth, Love, Spirit. His name is not just one or the other of these five expressions. For example, His Name is not just Truth. There can be no "Truth" without Love or intelligence. Neither is his Name "Love", though this title most closely expresses HIM. But Love without intelligence

Liberation

can be destructive. Witness the Earth Father of the flesh, buying his child ice cream cones and pop with "love". He does not have the wisdom (mind) to know that these things are extremely harmful because of the sugar and chemical additives contained within them. By this "love" he is actually laying the foundation for a sick child, and one or more of the degenerative diseases plaguing mankind today, later. This is a simple illustration of which you can think of many more, to know that Love alone is not sufficient . . . . Love must be balanced with Life, (reverence for) Mind, (intelligent use) Truth, (honest performance). As was said earlier, the balance of these four expressions of the Father will, and indeed MUST, raise one to SPIRIT.

"I AM" . . . . . The most powerful Affirmation on the Planet Earth at this time. When you can knowingly combine your "I AM" WILL with the conviction of WHO YOU ARE, then my Loved Ones, anything that you want to happen, will happen! Your soul does not belong to you, and you have seen how IT is the only REAL thing about you, so now . . . . Join yourself with

Liberation

the Father in an open declaration of UNION. "I AM HIS SOUL, HIS SOUL AND I ARE ONE". As the "Son of God" you are a part of the Power of the Father . . . . . you have only to realize this with your consciousness through MEDITATION and the assertion of The Great Affirmation to make this Great Truth Fact. You, who have read so far, realize now that the Whole Universe is the "Son of God". There was never a time when, "God sent his only Son". BUT, God does prevail THROUGH those who have managed to raise Their Vibration nearer to HIS POSITIVE LEVEL OF VIBRATION, through their own great effort. These "God like" Souls have walked the Earth as "Prophets" expressing God's Will at that time, to raise the prevailing Vibration. Their "Truth" was always the "bitter pill" of the times, and They generally suffered in the "hands of time" accordingly . . . . But not really "suffer". That was the "surface appearance". Behind every action about them they saw the "hand of God". So they could smile at the man who raised the hammer, or poured the burning oil. ALL is for a purpose. "NOTHING

Liberation

HAPPENS". Now that you understand the Law of Vibration you can readily "see" that their "message" may not be the "Word" for these "times" . . . . It was the "Truth" then . . . . And still is the "Truth" for some. There is no hard and fast "demarcation" line in Vibrations, However, In keeping with the Great law of Evolution, Old Truths become the Vibration which the New Vibration "stands upon" in order to balance itself while gathering its strength. Witness the Ten Commandments for This Age. Therein are all the old Commandments, but who cannot see the higher Vibration contained therein . . . . ? ALL IN KEEPING WITH THE PREVAILING LAW OF VIBRATION.

MEDITATION

MEDITATION

There are five ways of achieving the "Occult Powers". By Birth, by the Elixirs, by Penance, by Chanting, and by Meditation. This section of the Book deals with meditation, but perhaps a word should be said about the other four Keys to Power.

The followers of the Great Saints and "Saviors" of the Past were forgivably prone to exaggerate the prowess of their "Master" . . . . . to the point where in the cases where these Powers were actually possessed . . . . nothing would do, but that their Master had to be "born with them". To have their Master appear at all human would be untenable for this would place Him in the category of a "super-man" which is, after all, a step "below" the God they insisted upon making Him. Why? Because if they dared entertain the thought that "He" was just a man born of woman like himself, and raised himself to his great height by his own effect and will, you can see the burden that this kind of Understanding would bring to the follower.

Liberation

They would be challenged to perform in a similar manner as their idol. It is much easier to "worship" from a distance and idealize the man . . . . rather than his life. This places no direct responsibility upon the follower, for after all . . . . how could he possibly live by the same high "code" as a "God"?

In some cases the karma of the "Saint" is so good that these occult powers appear at a very early age, with very little effort on the part of the gifted one. But you can rest assured that in the previous life He earned every last "siddhi". So much for "Powers by Birth". But before we leave this subject perhaps the reader should know that one of the most misquoted, and misunderstood Masters in History studied for years with the Masters of the Far East in both Egypt and India. Fix this truth in your minds: "NOTHING COMES WITHOUT EFFORT". What is happening today, however, is that many with just a little effort are achieving unbelievably "fast results" . . . . but this is due to their "past efforts", and one of the primary

Liberation

purposes of the Book is to introduce these Great Saints and Sages of the past to themselves. Many need now only to reach a decision to first Master themselves, to become Master of ALL.

The "Elixirs" used and kept secret by the Ancient masters have vanished along with the old Initiation Rites; but then, as now, there was no "short cut" to God. The effects of the Drug taken were temporary. However . . . . there was one experience through a powerful drug that the initiate was given, which changed him permanently, and that was the actual experience of Death. After a given time the Initiate would be "brought back to life" and once having undergone the rite He would be fearless. As what fear can a man have who learns in this first hand manner that there is nothing to fear? . . . . He has been "there" and "knows" without doubt. Many today under the influence of LSD have had a glimpse of the "other worlds", the examples are too numerous to need mention here. You are all familiar with the "way out" trips, but all I can do is repeat my earlier

Liberation

warning that the risk is not worth the experience. LSD has served its purpose . . . . . now let it die a natural death.

"Penance" would mean, the exercise of severe disciplinary measures of living, such as in eating, sleeping, silence, comforts, etc. Some with no "guidance" from a Teacher have achieved the "Siddhis" in this way, showing that the forces respect, and will serve, the sincere Ones. Although this is the most difficult way, for sincerity is never really enough. There can be the greatest sincerity, but without wisdom and intelligent application, such "well meant" actions sometimes end in a mess!

"Chanting" is as old as Man, and the methods and manner of chanting have changed from age to age and from culture to culture. ALL chanting to God is good. ALL "mantras" are good. But some have the power of clarity and SOUND that can be likened unto a High powered Radio sending station that "cuts through" all interference, and reaches its objective, establishing a perfect channel

Liberation

between THE SOURCE and the RECEIVER. Other "stations" can have greatest sincerity, but their channel is weak, and their "sound" reaches the "receiver" indistinct, for the vibration is "weak" from age. ALL is Vibration, remember, so if you can generate a powerful dynamo of Energy within yourself by the sincere love of God, coupled with an intelligent understanding of just what it is you are chanting . . . . Your Vibration will penetrate through the Thought Dust (static), clearing a channel as it goes, gathering the "like" vibrations unto it as was explained earlier. As you know . . . . . Each Vibration is governed by the Law of the Circle, so You can readily see the inherent Power of chanting! If you couple your "chanting" with meditation your progress will be just as fast as your unfolding consciousness can bear it.

Now we come to the "Golden Key" that will unlock the doors of All Power . . . . . All Wisdom . . . . All Strength, and finally . . . . LIBERATION. ALL will be available to you who master Meditation . . . . below, as well as Above. It has been practiced by all men of all

Liberation

races and all times. It has been practiced by those who understand IT, but mostly by those who understand IT not. I am forced to smile at the different names given to meditation, such as Zen, Transcendental, etc. The unfolding neophyte is sometimes caught in this last trap which attempts to separate and divide mankind even at the very "Gate of Heaven"! Later, after experiencing true meditation, you can only "smile" with me at man's foolish attempts at "distinction" for the experience is the same for all . . . . and indeed MUST be the same, for It is the ultimate and final Earth Experience. "Those who, upon the moment of Death, have their attention fixed upon ME, COME STRAIGHT TO ME". It has been written.

Those who MASTER Meditation have it within their POWER to leave the body for a short time . . . . . Or for good. Many are the Saints and Sages who used this Power to leave the Body for the Last time under circumstances of violence or just "old age" . . . when they felt their usefulness in their present vehicle had ended.

Liberation

Any attempt at describing the experience of Meditation would prove futile. There is no way that words can be used to explain "what it is". All attempts to do so fall short of the actual experience. It would be like trying to explain the taste of honey to a man who had never tasted it. But notwithstanding my feeling of inadequacy for the task . . . . Let us make the attempt: by meditation man manages to raise his vibration from the physical to the mental, to the spiritual. His own center of Consciousness unfolds like the petals of a flower to the light of the Sun. His Vibration grows lighter and lighter until His BEING finally merges with the light, and there comes a moment when there is no difference between the "Light" and himself. There is "Light within, and Light without", and the Soul soars and expands to the very ends of the Universe. Gone are all feelings of Separateness. The Son has become one with the Father. A peace which "passeth all understanding" prevails. You become the Planets and Stars, their BEING passes through your Center without movement, for you ARE

Liberation

the Center, you ARE the circumference. Your body and mind dissolve in all that Light, and yet you are conscious of your own distinct identity throughout it all. Fear is discarded as an old useless garment, and when you return to the body your former feelings of Fear, Doubt, and inadequacy are gone, burned and dissolved by the Light of the Spirit. For these Earth "garments" of negativity cannot live within the Positive energy of the Absolute. The Positive will always destroy the negative. The Father is Above the Law of Opposites which hold man slave, and when man dares to approach His Light, All that is negative in man is destroyed, and the wounds from his Earthly experience healed. Such an experience cannot last for very long, or man would be dissolved in all the power, but it will happen just as often as You are able to "bear" IT. When the "Light" fades, do not try to hold it . . . . Spirit cannot be forced. Let it fade, and then bask in the warmth and Love of the Father. Gone are your "Questions", You "Know" now . . . . Not through reasoning or deducing, but through

Liberation

the experience of becoming ONE with ALL POWER and WISDOM. To have the experience once is enough for one lifetime, to be able to "enjoy" some part of that moment in time with the Father each morning is the greatest blessing the Father can bestow upon his deserving Son. The Spiritual Child has become the Spiritual Adult, ready and willing to help with the work of the Father. The "work" that is without effort, strain or pain, for now the Son understands ALL . . . . This brings an end to ATTACHMENT . . . . which in turn brings, LIBERATION. The "Fruits" of his labor belong to the Father. There is no "failure", there is no "success", there is just BEING! Peace and contentment reign within, and radiate without.

Now let us come down to Earth and learn the secrets of Meditation. Nothing pulls at the heartstrings more, of an Earthly Spiritual Father, than the sight of a Spiritual Child attempting to "meditate" without knowing how. This sad condition exists everywhere today for the "teachers" themselves do not know the "how" of meditation, or if they do know, they

Liberation

still feel bound by the Old Laws of the Masters, not to reveal the "method" to any except the "Chela" who has proven himself through his dedication. These "Laws" of secrecy were necessary during the past Ages for Man may have used the occult powers that come for negative purposes. Some did just that, and the black Magicians were created, bringing the downfall of more than one civilization such as Atlantis. But in this age these restrictions are no longer valid. Today the Spiritual Children are so scattered over the face of the Earth, that the only way "deserving" Souls can be reached now, is by the intelligent use of the channels available, such as this Book. No channel will go unused today, if it can be used to reach those who are crying out to the Father . . . . For no cry goes unheard . . . . No plea goes unanswered. Learn now, as Spiritual "Adults", to stop relating to "personalities". Begin now, to relate only to Truth, and you will find God speaking to you through the little child, the stranger, your "worst" enemy, a book, and on and on for the "channels" available to God are UNLIMITED.

Liberation

If you relate to personalities, or if you are still in the "bag" of judging, finding "fault", "criticizing", etc, You seal off the flow of one or more channels. Understand this now my Loved Ones. OPEN YOURSELF.

Meditation is Your Key that opens the door to the Spiritual World . . . . A world so beautiful that none, having once entered, want to ever leave . . . . . But there is work to be done, so, back all the Spiritually mature Ones must come. All is not "work" however, there is a time early in the morning before the day begins that has been "set aside" just FOR YOU. At that time the "channels" are the clearest, The "station" has been chosen . . . . . You turn yourself ON. For those who are ready . . . . this is the way to proceed:

After doing the Star Exercise in the manner described, Sit upon a skin, (It's alright . . . . The animal was killed for its meat and the skin is a by-product . . . . You might as well make use of it . . . . It is there) to help maintain the Vibrations within the body. The past masters of Meditation knew this secret, and so you will

Liberation

find them advising their students to "Sit upon a skin". You may face in any direction you choose, for none can face where God is not, but the important thing is to sit facing the same Focal Point each morning. So for this purpose you need an "Altar" in a quiet spot in the house. Your Altar should be colorful and inviting. The most necessary parts of your Altar are: A picture of a Man whom you feel to be "A Man of God". It can be any of the past or present Prophets. It can be an artist's conception of this man. The stipulations are only two: He Should be one who has never caused you doubt, disappointment or disillusionment, and his eyes should be looking straight at you.

There should be two or more candles lit around the picture. Of optional importance, but I feel very helpful, are "live" plants in pots and incense. The Posture you assume may be any, the important thing is that you sit without movement (even the slightest). One should sit as though "listening" with every fiber of One's Being, but relaxed. You may sit in a chair, or in Yogi fashion, in easy pose with the legs

Liberation

simply crossed, or "half lotus" with one foot tucked under the leg near the groin, and the other resting upon the opposite leg, or in full lotus, with both feet resting on the opposite thigh. Some find it useful to sit in one of the Yogi fashions for then he may sit "anywhere" where he may find himself and meditate, such as in Nature where no chairs are available. The only drawback to the Yoga postures is that the Western physique is ill prepared to sit comfortably for hours in one posture, whereas the Indian grew up sitting on the floor, and to him the floor is the same as a chair . . . . better in fact. But the body can be conditioned to anything, so if you have the fortitude and patience to condition yourself past the point of pain involved, the Eastern pose does have its advantages.

The "pose" you choose should be held for a minimum of thirty-six minutes. This is the usual time required before one enters the Meditative State. This also is where the greatest difficulty in Meditation lies, for it sometimes takes months to "transcend" the

Liberation

pain that surely comes after a short time in ANY posture. You may think that Meditating in a chair would be "easy" but you who have tried this know that after a time it becomes just as "painful" as any other posture, so as long as this is true, you might as will learn to Meditate in a Pose that "looks" as if you ARE Meditating. We all Influence by example . . . . which, after all, as you know, is the "best" way to teach. So, should a brother happen to notice you in meditation, perhaps it is best that he carry away with him the "proper" image. However, should you choose the "chair" or the "floor" the important thing is that you keep the Spine Erect and the chin comfortably held low. The hands should be resting relaxed on the knees. Your left palm up, and your right palm down. But before you begin Meditation, your physical and mental Vibrations are to be prepared in the following manner:

  Place your hands in your lap with the right thumb upon the pulse beat in your left wrist, and begin to count with the rhythm of the heart

Liberation

beat 1-2-3-4-5-6, then repeat the count until you feel the cadence perfectly. Then place the hands on the legs as described above and begin to breathe with that same rhythm six counts in, six counts holding the breath, six counts to exhale, six counts to hold the breath out. Then repeat until you feel "comfortable" with the flow. Now increase the beat to eight until you again feel relaxed into it, then to ten . . . . then to twelve counts. Always giving enough time to each "set" to become completely comfortable in the doing. It may take you a little while to reach twelve. Stop at the count that seems to be accompanied with a very "special" breath. I know of no other way to express this. At this time inhale deep, and allow your exhale to "fall" without thought of effort . . . . Now, without thinking of inhaling (do not strain to hold the breath out . . . . inhale when you must) concentrate your full attention upon the eye (it can be either) of your "desired Deity" in front of you. Think of nothing except holding your attention upon the Eye. When the mind wanders, bring it back, again and again, to that

Liberation

point of concentration. When you are able to fix your mind without wavering upon the "Eye" for twelve seconds, you will have achieved "concentration". This will give you some idea how difficult (at first) this exercise is to do. Don't give up . . . "Perseverance furthers". Hold your concentration without blinking or shifting the eyes until the eyes begin to water . . . at this time . . . close the eyes and "contemplate" the "third Eye point" (is a realization beginning to flash you?) at the top of the forehead. Breathe when you MUST, otherwise, hold out without effort or strain. Sit without movement of the eyes, hands or feet, and try to reproduce the picture that is in front of you in your mind's eye. It will want to fade away . . . Other thoughts will push their way into your mind, and each time this happens you must, "slay the slayer of the Real" . . . . . Eventually the mind will be yours. If you would slay the enemy that rushed from the Castle you were trying to take, one by one, as they emerged . . . . . there would come a time when there was no one left in the fortress, and

Liberation

the Castle would fall to YOU. practice this exercise for 36 minutes the first week, and increase the time of practice by six minutes a week until you can sit for One and a half hours without movement. After this accomplishment (and you are to be congratulated, for this is quite an accomplishment), You can increase the time according to your own desire and needs. it has been written that three hours is necessary. In this Age of Speed, I doubt the necessity of this, but it still might "feel right" for some . . . so do what you will.

There will come a time when through your developed "one-pointedness of mind" you will pass beyond the "face" and into the LIGHT. From that time on you need no longer "go through" the eye of your "Deity" to meditate. Keep your attention on the changing shades of forms and light, and allow the Vibration to take you Higher and Higher into the pure White Light.

You now have within your grasp the secret of the "Third Eye". this is the "Eye" that will lead you into the Light. That "World" that seems

Liberation

now so distant, but within which, we move and live, and have our BEING. UNTIL YOU BEGIN TO RELATE TO THINGS "UNSEEN" .... THE THINGS THAT ARE "SEEN" WILL HOLD YOU WITHIN THEIR VIBRATION. Man will always, and indeed MUST, become whatever it is his attention is focused upon. Such is the Law. Each is his own Creator and Destroyer. His own Heaven and Hell.

In a very short time you will discover that during those moments (at first "success" is measure by moment) when you succeed in forgetting all else except the desired point of concentration .... You will have forgotten to breathe, and you will be brought back with a "start" at this discovery. You are on your way ..... You have entered the "stream", you now have only to immerse yourself completely. When you achieve this moment, forget yourself entirely (try) and make an effort to "hold" the picture steady in front of you (still concentrating at the top of the head and with the eyes closed). Sooner or later the "Light"

Liberation

will come, and with it a new "Birth" for you. You will know what it means to be "re-born while Living". The beautiful thing about Meditation is that one does not have to wait for the "ultimate" experience without rewards along the way. Each Meditation brings some "Light", and always just the amount that you can bear. A great Master once said, "I have many things to teach you, but you cannot bear to hear them yet". Similarly, if you could receive the Light, "all at once", you would not be able to "bear it".

Now, My Loved Ones, You have reached the level of awareness where you can be told ALL without reservation. The next step from here is to strengthen your Vibration to a point where you will be able to "bear" the Light of God. Many are those who were ill prepared for the experience, who shrank from the Light as if it were a ghostly specter, and so lost out on the most sought after experience known in the Occult. Spirit cannot be hurried, for it moves at a pace in keeping with the "capacity" of the "vehicle". Know that you are progressing as

Liberation

you should, and leave the rest up to THE GREAT LAW. Be cheered by the thought that, "failure is impossible"..... success is assured. What is time anyway, other than "objects" used for measuring distance by Earth Standards? Time is unthinkable without "things" and "happenings" to measure with. In the Eternity time does not exist..... there is only the ever present. NOW, for ALL is ONE, AND ONE IS ALL. Fix this thought in your consciousness until it becomes part of your very BEING.

At the close of your Meditation, extend both legs forward and reach to the farthest-most point you are able and, keeping the knees stiff, stretch the "life nerve" which runs down either side of your legs. Try to hold this position until the "pain turns to pleasure". Stretching this nerve, every morning will keep you young and supple throughout life.

Now resume your Meditation pose and with your heart filled with the Love of God, sing out "THE GREAT AFFIRMATION" and listen for the entire Universe to join in your praise. How long you should chant is up to you. Chant as

Liberation

long as it feels right. One Master claims that it is possible to achieve Liberation if you chant for 2-1/2 hours every morning before the rising of the Sun for 30 days. Such is the Power of Vibration. Whichever method, and time you choose, the important thing is to stay with it, and pay heed to the advice from "The Secret Doctrine" . . . . . "Resist Change".

For you who have trouble finding your Center and your mind refuses to remain still, even for the twelve seconds necessary to achieve concentration, there is a very Powerful way by which you can "Zero In" on the REAL YOU. Sit erect in Meditation pose, close the eyes, inhale deep, and with your very last breath repeat your first name over and over again steadily and somberly, Begin each "set" with the prefix, "I AM" . . . . . Repeat the procedure for as long as it takes to put you in touch with your Center. It should not take very long before "help" comes . . . . Remember my Loved Ones, YOU ARE NOT ALONE.

I must tell you, so that, when you have the experience, you will not "freak out" . . . . there

Liberation

will come a time in the above exercises or possibly, one of the others, when you will "feel" your extremities "dissolving" followed by the rest of the body . . . . . At that time, have courage, fear stops any phenomena, relax into it, and forget the self. All of the experiences you will have are for the PURPOSE OF ENCOURAGING YOU ON THE PATH . . . . . To let you know that you are moving along as you should. Do not get "hung up" with the "happenings" for this can be a trap for the ego. It does not matter who you were in your past Life, or what your "vision" was this morning, etc. Beware of the most insidious "trap" of ALL . . . . SPIRITUAL EGO. It has cost more than One Soul the price of a return ticket. How can there be ego, when you know we are All One? Your brother's "success", is your "success" . . . . . his, "failure" is your "failure". But if you see either success or failure . . . . . you understand it not.

The very "best" time to Meditate is in the early morning before the Dawn. However, any time is a "good" time, provided you do not

Liberation

neglect your Earthly obligations. Do not make the mistake that so many make on the Path . . . . They find a little Spirituality and, in the fear of (I suppose) losing it, they neglect to come down and get their Earth trip together. These spaced out Spiritual Children can be seen everywhere today. The Obeying of the First and Second Commandments prevents this, but of course, as was said earlier . . . . Love cannot be commanded. So you can see how important it is that you find your Earthly Spiritual Father. "Seek, and Ye shall find" . . . . . This is both a promise and a Law. If you keep your ego, i.e., not give it to another, you will remain in the same fix as the tadpole who can only live in water until it loses its tail, then it can live in either the water or the land as it chooses . . . . . Similarly the neophyte can only live on the Earth until he loses his ego (gives to another), and then he can live either on the Earth, or whenever he chooses, he may "dive into the ocean of spiritual bliss" and escape the oppressive Earth Vibration.

It does no good to tell someone that "they

Liberation

should give up the ego". That is like saying one should give up the "jumping mind". Both will die a natural death from observing the commandments and Meditating. For both are dependent for their survival upon the belief in separateness. Once union with the Divine is experienced, All sense of separateness goes. The fearlessness of those who have achieved this Union is sometimes mistaken for "Ego" by the unaware. But a close look, will reveal to the objective critic, that this man of God . . . . . is only "selling" God. By the same token, those who have not had the illuminating experience are easily recognized in the fanatic, with his little truth . . . . . And the "holy man" with hand out.

With these words this section on Meditation comes to an end. The "secrets" that were revealed to you were given by Divine Inspiration. This marks the first appearance in print of some of the most carefully guarded secrets of the Masters. If you will be helped by what has been revealed, and if you use your unfolding powers for the good of Humanity,

Liberation

you will take your place alongside the world Saviors of All ages. You are the "Salt of the Earth". The leaven that will lighten the load of All humanity that follows . . . . . May God bless You, and shower His Light upon You.

THE 8 STEPS NECESSARY

RESTRAINT:
> Harmlessness to all living things.

OBSERVANCES:
> Keeping the Universal Laws, Chanting.

POSTURE:
> Steady, for one hour

BREATH CONTROL:
> Holding out.

ABSTRACTION:
> Withdrawal of mind from the senses.

CONCENTRATION:
> Complete attention for twelve seconds.

MEDITATION:
> Union with the Father.

ABSORPTION:
> Wholly occupied and involved with Spirit.

THE 9 IMPEDIMENTS

DISEASE:
    Any departure from health.

DEBILITY:
    Weakness or feebleness of the body.

DOUBT:
    Uncertainness of Belief.

INADVERTENCE:
    Non-attention . . . Distraction

SLOTH:
    Indolence, lack of exertion.

SENSUALITY:
    Indulging the senses.

NON-ATTAINMENT:
    Discouragement over lack of achievement.

INSTABILITY:
    Lack of firmness or steadiness.

PERVERSE KNOWLEDGE:
    Wrong information

CONCLUSION

"AND, NOW, OH TEACHER OF COMPASSION POINT THOU THE WAY TO OTHER MEN. BEHOLD, ALL THOSE WHO ARE KNOCKING FOR ADMISSION, AWAIT IN IGNORANCE AND DARKNESS, TO SEE THE GATE OF THE SWEET LAW FLUNG OPEN!"

TEACH WHAT YOU HAVE RECEIVED FOR YOU NOW STAND MASTER OF THE PROBATIONARY PATH. THE TIME TESTED ROAD OF THE DISCIPLE LOOMS AHEAD, STEEP AND THORNY WITH PITFALLS AT EVERY TURN TO TRAP AND ENSNARE THE WEARY PILGRIM. AT EACH BEND IN THE ROAD A MAN MUST FACE HIMSELF. ONLY THE INNOCENT ONES ARMED WITH LOVE AND FAITH ARE SAFE, HELD SECURELY IN THE BOSOM OF THE FATHER.

AS BELOW, SO ABOVE,
                        AS ABOVE, SO BELOW.

An Update to

LIBERATION

This reprinting of the original text was printed in February of 2004, and includes a brief overview of the life of Jim Baker / Father Yod / Ya Ho Wha, The Source Family and selected, important Wisdom

TABLE OF CONTENTS

I - LIBERATION – The Book – in its original form – *ABOVE*

II - Introduction to this 2003 update
A brief overview of the life of Jim Baker, Father, Father Yod and Ya Ho Wha and His Source Family

III - Father's Legacy

IV - The Age of Aquarius

V - "The Ancient and Sacred Name of God"
 ▓▓▓▓▓ Yod He Vau He / Ya Ho Wha
 1) Introduction to "The Name"
 2) Compilation of facts and ideas
 3) Detailed Analysis

VI – How to Die Rightly

VII - AND what might this ALL mean to me?

II ~ Introduction
To the 2004 Reprinting

Jim Baker, Father, Father Yod and Ya Ho Wha . . . and His Source Family

Ya Ho Wha was a man who was born James E. Baker, on July 4, 1922. This is a very brief overview of the extraordinary story of Jim Baker – and of his evolution into "Father Yod" and then **Ya Ho Wha** – and his spiritual Family, The Source Family, who knew him as "Father". There were close to 100 of us who stayed with him - as much as we could - for the last few years of his life on this Earth.

Jim's Father, Jim Baker, left him and his mother when Jim was only about 6 months old. Jim Baker spent the rest of his very eventful and inspirational life, Searching for his Father – or at least a "Father Figure". This search lead him to seek "The Truth" - from all faiths, philosophies, earthly and Spiritual Paths. This was his life quest. He eventually recognized Yogi Bhajan as his Spiritual Father. Jim went to India with the Yogi and – when someone asked him if he were Hindu or Sikh – he threw his Sikh headdress into the Ganges River, and said: "Neither a Hindu nor a Sikh will I be . . . for my soul is universal and free !" This started his transition into another level of Spiritual awareness . . . into the "New Age" vibration. Father always said that the next spiritual awakening would not be from the East, but from the West.

Jim opened the Source Restaurant – on Sunset Boulevard – in 1969. This was one of the country's first health food restaurants. His own "Spiritual Family" grew from among those working at the Source and those who were drawn to him through his meditation classes. We sold The Source in 1974, and it stayed open until 2000, a Hollywood legend and tradition for 31 years.

The group – or Family – that was growing up around this incredible being soon came to be known as "The Brotherhood of the Source." We called him "Father", because we recognized him as our "Earthly Spiritual Father". He began the Religion of Ten (The Eternal Now), and we soon became "The Source Family" – living communally in the Hollywood Hills. The Source Family was not a "Religion" that one could simply join . . . it was just a "Family" of good people who lived together, worked together and were inexorably drawn to each other, and to Father. In these early years of the family, Father "Channeled" this book, "LIBERATION", in 10 days. It was written in the energy of the early 1970's and well before many of his greatest Teachings and insights "Came down" to us. Reading some of this book — now — it will be clear that we were living in an entirely different era of history and yet . . . most of these teachings are so profound that they still occupy a major place in the consciousness of many . . . Timeless Wisdom.

Jim Baker / Father Yod's intense desire for the elusive "Truth" led him ultimately to the essence of western esoteric teachings: the Kabala and the Tetragrammaton. The Tetragrammaton has been called the great, unspeakable "Name of God" for at least four millennia. If Truth be told . . . it is really just the initials of that Name and — although it appears upon the entrances of all the great stone churches and cathedrals of the middle ages — the pronunciation and the meaning of "The Name" have been carefully hidden by the few who were taught this sacrosanct information. Therefore it has been largely lost to modern Christianity, except in diluted form, through secret societies, rare or out-of-print books, some oral tribal teachings and Freemasonry and other secret societies. Father Yod "Channeled" the true pronunciation of The Name . . . and he was the first (and -- for a long time) the only person who gave it openly and freely ! With Father's guidance, we began to chant the Name of God: **Yod Heh Vau Heh, Ya Ho Wha, Ya Ho Wha Ho**.

He always said, if you want to get someone's attention, call him by name.

He taught us that there is great Power in *any word* . . . but exceptionally in *"The Word"* ! Thus, we began our real spiritual growth — as a Family — founded upon "The Ancient NAME of God." And the forms that issued from it followed the great, creative formula that is the Name: Yod Heh Vau Heh. Father, Mother, Union . . . Issue — FIRE, WATER, AIR and EARTH. The Name is dynamic, living and instructive in the processes of life — everywhere in the universe — and still sacred beyond the understanding of most people. There are several different illuminations of "The Name" in the section below, written and compiled to help you on this Path, by various Members of The Source Family.

In late 1974, Father Yod took the name YA HO WHA" — in honor and Remembrance of the ancient and Sacred Name of God. Thus . . . after an exhaustive, lifelong search — Jim Baker . . . Ya Ho Wha — actually attained "God Consciousness" — while still in His "Earthly Body". He realized that his destiny was to tell us that we also — as men and women of this age, have the ability and destiny to also attain that Consciousness.

Although our time with him was short . . . we all held our Father in such reverence — and the Wisdom and Love that he gave to us all was so profound – that our perspective was to look up to him as an exalted being. We all were literally fed by his energy. Although he often warned us not to accept what he said as gospel, but to figure out the truth for ourselves, as a group, we tended to unquestioningly accept what he said and did. He bestowed Teachings upon us that came – not only from his own life experience and wisdom – but also from many other sources. He tried to distill the "Wisdom of the Ages" for us, passing to us jewels of Truth from many traditions.

He was a profound teacher. Each "Morning Class" was an awesome, Life-Changing Experience unto itself, during which each of us absorbed hundreds of thousands of calories of energy from his power and Wisdom. Each one took away that which his physical, mental and Spiritual strength enabled him to. For some, the Teachings were profound. Others ran from his presence in fear. For the few who could *truly hear Him* . . . they will never be the same and they find that – even 30 years later – their feet have been turned to a path that leads them beyond any consciousness of which they could otherwise have ever dreamed!

Although he used many of the Teachings from the Yogi, he drew Truths from many diverse philosophies and spiritual paths and had a lot of his own "Flashes". Heavy Teachings began to "Come Down" through him. This was before most people spoke of "Channeling". He often spoke of opening up to the "Akashic Records".

One of the most revolutionary concepts that he introduced into The Family was the liberation of all women. He raised women up as "God's first creation," and called each one "The Mother of All Living". He respected and honored the feminine / goddess energy long before others did and encouraged woman to freely express her soul as the creative force of the universe.

The Women created the unions within the Family, and always had free choice when it came to choosing which of Ya Ho Wha's Suns they vibrated to. Father taught us that a God Man should be passive in such matters, not showing preference or pursuing any particular Woman. He taught that His Sons should be one-pointed into God, and that any Woman who came to him, should be graciously accepted as a gift from God, without judgment.

In August of 1975, Father left his earthly body. The Family was living in Hawaii and numbered over 100 people, with a council of Father's 13 women. In the early years Father had specifically asked that we gather as a Family on "September 17, 2001" . . . for the transition into the "Golden Age". So, 26 years later, we held a big Family reunion on the

Hawaiian Island of Oahu – which resulted in the forming of "The Source Foundation" . . . and a new bonding of "The Family", after many years.

It is in tribute to Jim Baker . . .

Ya Ho Wha

~ Our Earthly Spiritual Father ~

that we are reprinting this book ... presenting it in the original form – and adding this update.

III – FATHER'S LEGACY

Father taught us many things. Four of His Key Teachings were:

1 - How to "Live Rightly" – His Teachings included clear guidance on how to obtain ultimate health (including conscious, natural childbirth, breast feeding, the best possible diet, exercises, meditation, chanting and the constant use of the Sacred Breath) and a fundamental respect for the Laws of Nature and The Sacred Teachings.

2 - How to "Die Rightly" – He taught us that the Body – from which the Soul was departing – should be undisturbed and surrounded by loved ones for 3 ½ days, with no embalming, autopsy or blood transfusions . . . for all memory is contained in the blood. This allows time for the body elements to shut down, time for one to view their "River of Life" in full consciousness and time for the Spirit to acknowledge the Earthly bonds, and to let go of them. The ultimate visualization for those surrounding the body would be to chant the ancient name of God during that time.

3 - How to "Do Business Rightly" – To "Maintain

the Standard", to do every act with "Life, Mind, Truth, Love and Spirit", to leave any energy better than the way you found it, to be honest and fair, to be on time, etc.

4 - To Come to Know the Meaning of – and the Power of – to Resurrect, restore and give freely – and to Sing – **THE ANCIENT** (and heretofore hidden) **AND SACRED NAME OF GOD** . . .

YOD HE VAU HE . . . YA HO WHA HO
YHVH YHWH
[numerically "Digits" (totals) 26]

Fire, Water, Air and Earth

We are a tribal Family, founded on "God's Name" – The Name that GOD himself gave – from the beginning of time – for the 140, the 4000 and the 144,000 "Children of the Light" – as "HIS" witness.

He gave us these "Keys" to help us ascend – on the **Physical** – as well as the **Spiritual** – plane.

"Lose memory ~ lose all !"

"I am You and You are Me ~
so it exists for Eternity".

IV – THE AGE OF AQUARIUS

Without a vision . . . The people will perish !

We now enter "The Age of Aquarius" . . .

The age of Light ! The age of Reason !

The age of Communication and Understanding !

The GOLDEN AGE !!!

Many remember the song: "This is the dawning of the Age of Aquarius". Most people don't realize that WE ARE IN THAT AGE . . . now ! This is a very real phenomenon that is coming to pass right as this is being written.

Of course — astronomical and astrological transitions take time. Major transitions don't usually happen suddenly. It takes a few days to move from Pisces into Aries each year. Can you imagine how many days it may take to move

FROM the Age of Pisces (which is the weighty, deep, cold Age of Water) . . . INTO The Age of Aquarius . . . ? We are definitely in those days (or years) of transition, during which our precious little

"PLANET, GODDESS, EARTH", is moving into **THE AGE OF AQUARIUS.**

Father always said that the actual date of transition was

September 17th, 8:00 pm, 2001.

Does this mean that we can expect things to suddenly change dramatically. Well, doesn't that always seem to be the case – no matter what ? But – to some degree – that is up to you. What are "YOU" . . . going to do . . . with YOUR "GOLDEN AGE" ?

V – The NAME / The WORD

1) Introduction –

One very important **"Key"** – that Father gave us and which will serve us well to remember – is to make sure that we clearly comprehend the fact that **"Words have great power"** !   Father often said that Words do not stop at walls, or city limits, or any other limits . . . that Each Word – indeed – travels all the way around the World . . . and comes back to recognize – and therefore AFFECT – the person who used the Word in the first place.

When we finally come to understand this . . . we realize that we can make our "Path" much easier if we learn to be exquisitely careful of what we say . . . because we <u>literally create our own reality by our choice of the Words that we use</u> !

Are you "_Sick_" ?   Or are you "_Improving_" ?
Do you "_Hate your job_" ?
Or are you "_Striving for a better position_" ?

Words are the active powers of the God within us . . . used for good or ill . . . !
It's our choice . . . .

Words are more critical to the mind . . .
than light is to the eyes !

And there is **ONE WORD** . . .

which has been known for untold thousands of years !

This "Word" proved to be so powerful . . . that very few ever even knew of its existence ! The knowledge of this "Word" was meticulously HIDDEN ! Only a handful of the Members of the "Inner Sanctums" of MOST – IF NOT ALL – of the World's "Faiths" were even told of this Sacred Key . . . and they were sworn to the most severe secrecy . . . And almost NO ONE was allowed to speak it. The speaking of "The Name" was limited to one priest, in each Temple

— ONCE A YEAR — where no one could hear him! And, while he was actually speaking The Name — he would cover up the sound by playing the gong!

The few who were allowed to know of its existence at all, were allowed to call it by its Hebrew initials ONLY . . . "Yod Heh Vau Heh"! Even in *this form*, this is the Most Sacred Word known to Man. Most other Western faiths held on to their versions of it . . . sort of variations upon a theme . . . like "Yeheshua", "Yahweh", "Jehovah", etc.

All it means is . . . .
    Fire! Water!! Air!!! and Earth!!
    Everything that we are made of . . .
    All that *everything* is made of!
    And it means   "I am that . . . I am."

As innocent and beautiful as it seems, you may or may not be amazed to know, that there are some people who will be outraged . . . even enraged . . . with us for telling you this!

In the next two sections, you will be given a

fairly detailed and comprehensive analysis of This Word. It has been written (and / or compiled) for you by original Source Family Members.

This graphic illustrates how "This Word" has been written for four millennia . . . It is Hebrew and is read from right to left.

"YA HO WHA"

Is the actual pronunciation of this "WORD" . . . This "NAME".

IN THE BEGINNING WAS THE WORD AND *THE WORD WAS GOD*.

. . . THE LOGOS, THE WORD

the eternal, life-giving principal of the universe.

ALL SECRET WISDOM IS HIDDEN IN NUMBER.

The Eternal "**Akashic Records**" contain the first pulsations of **God, in creation** – which manifest as Light – the **"Supreme, Creative *"WORD"*, in which all things are fashioned.**

This is "just" information. But – be under no illusions . . . The Name is more than **magical**, greater than **powerful** . . . indeed . . . it is <u>*Wisdom*</u>. And . . . If you can hear this . . . And if you care . . . You <u>*may want to use*</u> the power of "This Sacred Word" . . . To help realize your own ascension ! On the physical . . . as well as on the spiritual plane.

If God truly is omnipresent . . . ? Then . . . ?

Father always said, "If you want to get someone's attention . . . call him BY NAME !"

V – The NAME / The Word

2) Sacred Commentary

"<u>Y H V H</u>" is the Ineffable four-lettered "Name of God", known as

"The TETRAGRAMMATON" !

It appears exactly 6,832 times in the original Old Testament, known as the Scriptures. It is held to possess unbounded power, sufficient – it is said – to shake the very foundations of Heaven and Earth. The study of the "Ancient scripts or scrolls" will help us to resonate with the vibration of this "Fiery, Encoded Living Language of Light."

The purpose of decoding the Old Testament is to clarify the "Sacred Names" and to show how the higher spiritual teachings of the ancients also revealed prophecies of the future. They did this by emphasizing the deeper meaning, and going beyond the allegorical and symbolic levels, which had historically been used to keep the message hidden. They reveal the "Spoken meaning", that binds humanity into a cosmic order of greater dimensions than ever believed . . . "In the beginning was the Word and the Word was God, and made Holy" !

God has a name and it is to be invoked ! God wrote this "NAME" for Moses, in the stone tablets of the Ten Commandments, which are kept in the Ark of the Covenant. These four Hebrew letters — when written — form the Tetragrammaton, and are to be read from right to left. Represented, in English, as <u>YHVH / YHWH.</u> The first language used in writing the Bible was Hebrew, and — when the Hebrew language was written — the writers wrote only consonants . . . not vowels. Hence, for God's name, they did the same thing and wrote only the consonants.

The pronunciation of "The Name" was familiar to the Israelites so, when they saw it in this abbreviated form, they knew how it sounded in their minds. As, if we were to read "bldg." . . .

we would know it was building. The Jewish people also believed it was wrong to pronounce the name "God" or "Lord" and you will often see written "G---" and "L---".

But, it is difficult to imagine why it was considered so wrong to use the true name of God . . . since it appears in original Hebrew Texts 6,832 times ! In the second half of the first millennium, Jewish scholars invented a system of points to represent the missing vowels. They placed these around the consonants in the Hebrew Bible. This was to ensure that the pronunciation of the Hebrew Language, as a whole, would not be lost. However, in reference to God's name, they put other vowel signs to remind the reader that they should say "Adhonai". Then came the spelling Iehouah and, eventually, Jehovah, which became the accepted pronunciation of the divine name in English. Yahweh came from a form suggested by modern scholars, who were trying to clarify the original pronunciation.

In times past, God's name (in the form of the Hebrew Tetragrammaton) was used on many Religious buildings. You can find it still on many stained glass windows or plaques on churches in France, Germany and Spain . . . you can find it on statues at the Vatican, as well as in several of the paintings from the "Masters". There is also a German coin from 1661, with the Hebrew letters of YHVH on it, in a German Museum.

Yod He Vau He on a statue at the Vatican

The Divine Name – in many forms – has endured throughout the ages, as the servants of God kept on honoring his name. In the third century BC an effort was made to translate the Old Testament into Greek, the new international language of the times. The translators did not put in the true Name . . . but rather wrote it in the Hebrew form of the YHVH (which became the standard way that the Sacred Name was hidden from the masses). It is not known when God's Name was no longer spoken aloud by the Jewish people, but about that same time, they began to substitute the Hebrew letters of this "Tetragrammaton".

The name passed out of everyday use well before Jesus' time, but the apostles went forth and did give the name. Let your name be sanctified ! And the high priest – once a year, on the "Day of Atonement" – would pronounce it rightly, in the inner temple, with the sounding of the gong (so no one else could hear). This was done until the temple was destroyed in 70 BC. The name eventually got removed from copies and translations of the Bible, when they translated the original Hebrew and Greek to other languages. The YHVH was replaced with "Lord". The King James Version states the word "Jehovah" does not accurately represent any form of the name ever used in Hebrew . . . and so it uses Lord or God.

Over a period of time, the Hebrew people chose not to use The Sacred Name – in their daily lives or even in the Temples. But they still did not remove it from most of their ancient texts, including the older manuscripts of the Bible. Hence the Hebrew Scriptures still contain God's name. Before long, the Divine Name was lost to the Gentile Church, as well, except where it was remembered by scholars. The Jews refused to pronounce it and the Christian Church managed to remove it completely.

The Hebrew males, under their clothing, were commanded to wear the four fringes (called tzitzit) as a reminder of the name of God. They are tied with knots in such a way as to spell the Name of YHVH. The non-orthodox Jew later began to only wear them when they prayed and so made them part of what is now the prayer shawl, or tallis. When the Hebrew letter "Shin" is added in the center of YHVH, the Name of the Father becomes the Name of the son.

YHSVH – Yod He Shin Vau He – "JESUS".

THIS IS THE HEBREW YHSVH ~(YOD HE SHIN VAU HE) ~ FORMING THE SON OF THE FATHER, JESUS. THE SHIN -MEANS FIRE IN THE MIDDLE, THE HEART.

<u>YHVH</u> is the way this "Word" has been written for millennia. However, most people still said Yeheshua, Yahweh or Jehovah.

THIS IS YHVH ~ (YOD HE VAU HE) ~ IN HEBREW~ FORMING MAN OUT OF THE IMAGE OF THE FATHER IN HIS NAME. (THE HEAD, THE TORSO WITH THE ARMS, THE BODY, THE HIPS AND THE LEGS.)

CUNEIFORM OF THE NAME
(this is the way YHVH was written before the Hebrew)

"There are many ways being used to write and pronounce the Name, the Tetragrammaton. But... in the end, what is important is to "Live it and become it".

YHWH/YHVH is the Eternal Name. It is the blueprint of the keys for our understanding of the evolutionary track of the Universe. To know and use this Name is to stop being Wisdom-keepers and become Wisdom sharers. To witness in a way that truly raises inner consciousness and brings about global awakening of a positive future.

The Original Hebrew, Greek and Aramaic Scrolls can be followed in "The New World Translation of the Holy Scriptures", where the name **YHVH** is restored.

The Holy Name, The Jerusalem and The Schofield Bible editions are also Recommended.

V – The NAME / The Word

3) In Depth Review

The human race is now entering the Aquarian Age; which is to be an age of global enlightenment, communications and equity. Aquarius is the zodiacal sign of "knowing." What this means is that the natural, next phase of our survival, as the human species, is to **"Create A More Perfect Union"** between the individual parts of our **"Species Body", by "Knowing The Truth That Will Set You Free."**

There are an infinite number of things one can know about, but none is more important than the knowing of who – and what – you are, and this is why the ancient words, spoken by the sages, are **"Know Thyself And Thou Shall Know All."**

So, brothers and sisters, what is there to know about one's self – which is also to be known about "The all" . . . and be set free ? What is this mysterious, elusive knowledge that is common to all – and one, at the same time – and how do you come to understand and know it ?

To deliver this knowledge is the very reason we – of the great "Religion of **T.E.N**", "The Eternal Now," are – at this cosmic moment in time – heralding the shifting of the consciousness of mankind between the ages. We are called upon, by our Heavenly Father, to bring forth to the mind of humanity the concise revelation of the "Divine Intelligence" of the most ancient and Sacred Name of God.

This "Name" was written 3600 years ago, in the Hebrew flame language of living light, and was sent forward in time to when the human race would once again speak in one language, which happens to be English. The English alphabet – even the word "Alphabet" itself – finds its source in the 22 Hebrew letters, beginning with it's first two, Aleph and Beth {the Greek coming on the scene 1000 years later, with Alpha Beta}. This alphabet was very consciously constructed by initiated beings, whose high degree of intelligence and knowledge of sacred geometry and math could be – for all intents and purposes – considered "Angelic", or "Of the angels", or

Angel-ish. So, if "English" is "Of the angels", or even of the angles (which are "Aspects drawn between the planets and constellations of the Heavens, where Angels 'live"), then Hebrew – from which English stems – contains the original meaning that English was intended to convey.

Thus we return to "The Source" – Hebrew – where we find (waiting there for centuries) the knowing and the knowledge that can illuminate and cause a reunification of the individual, scattered, "parts" of the human species, who seek and find this specific knowledge. From its understanding and usage, "We, the people of YHVH" – the Human Race – can and will know who we are, and live as one.

The knowledge of which I speak is contained within the sound, shape, meaning and number of the 4 letters – YHVH – which, in Hebrew, are called YOD HEH VAU HEH, and pronounced YA HO WHA – being the numbers 10-5-6-5. Hebrews used their letters to represent both letters and numbers. This allows us (as well) to derive deep, hidden, universal Truths – from reality – which strengthens our interrelationships with ourselves and our environments.

The English, King James version of the Old Testament disguised this 4 lettered name of God with the word "Lord", or — just as misleading — with Jehovah, and the anthropomorphic concept. By this means, the "Common people" of 1000 years ago, who were just learning to read and write through the Bible, were collectively prevented from surely and exactly knowing the divine and personal communication in the Name. It was to know that, "YOU ARE CREATED IN THE IMAGE AND LIKENESS OF GOD, BOTH WOMAN AND MAN" and that "DIVINE UNITY IS OUR GOAL" for "GOD IS ONE".

The literal, grammatical meaning of these 4 Letters — in Hebrew, as written — is the conjugation of the verb "TO BE" or IS . . . WAS and WILL BE. {This most ancient "Name of God" is therefore an action **verb** and definitely not a **proper noun**} Another way of saying this is "THE ETERNAL". Furthermore . . . if you take the numbers of YHVH, 10-5-6-5, and add them together they "Digit" 26, the number of parts of a cube [the Hebrew Letters are sometimes called "the cubic letters"], and the number of letters used in the English alphabet, which can then be reduced to the simpler number 8, which means Eternity and Infinity.

The YOD, or Y, is 10, the number of completeness, and represents the soul plane, coming forth into our personalities, when we allow this to happen. The intended completeness of our Being – YHVH – waits for us to turn from outer to inner consciousness; towards the soul's emanations, receiving It's divine qualities. This book, "LIBERATION", is the "Quick path", preparing you to receive your soul emanations.

Now, here's the big secret which even those who know Hebrew don't know . . . if you take these 4 letters and place them vertically one upon the other – in their Hebrew shapes – [**see the diagram at the end of this section**] you can easily see the silhouette of a human being, revealing the message that "**You [Soul Essence] Are That Which Is Eternal, Unlimited and Perfect**" right now.

Being eternal and infinite is like YHVH saying there is no death and that we will come again to continue this mission to free our minds from the illusion of separation which has been caused by the absorption of man's consciousness in the sole experience of pleasure and pain . . . in the 5 senses, third dimensional realm.

The path from the "fall" of Consciousness absorbed in the physical dimension of apparent separateness from every other thing, to enlightenment and conscious, union and love with All, is called **"The Ascension"** and this too is shown in the Name YHVH, standing vertically. The path begins from the H below, representing the great physical plane, through the upper 3 letters, V H and Y, which stand for the immediate, inward dimensions of the Emotional-Mental and Soul Planes, respectively.

The Ascension is within and requires 4 stages; PURIFICATION OF THE BODY by Mastery of the 5 Senses, REFINEMENT OF THE EMOTIONS by the Mastery of Speech, ELEVATION OF THE MIND by the Mastery of Thought and LIBERATION OF THE SOUL by service to Humanity.

Together these 4 stages are called "**THE UNIFICATION AND SANCTIFICATION OF THE HOLY NAME**". What this actually means is for you to unify your own physical-emotional-mental and spiritual dimensions within and sanctify them, so that their symphony of unique vibrations can never again be at contrary purposes. One by one – and as one – the human race will ascend and transform the Earth back into "Heaven".

The 4 lettered Word, which represents the 4 imminent dimensions of our nature, also represents the Nature of All that exists on all planes and dimensions of Being in that it represents the Divine Law of 4 as 1, shown in the explanation below:

In the elemental realm . . .
    FIRE WATER AIR EARTH

In the table of elements . . .
OXYGEN HYDROGEN NITROGEN CARBON

In the personal realm . . .
    WILL MIND EMOTION BODY

In the human/animal realm . . .
    FATHER MOTHER SON DAUGHTER

In the genetic realm . . .
ADENINE CYTOSINE GUANINE THYMINE

In the musical realm . . .
MELODY HARMONY RHYTHM TEMPO

In the astrological realm . . .
LEO SCORPIO AQUARIUS TAURUS

In the numerical realm . . .
$$1 + 2 + 3 + 4 = 10 = 1$$
$$4 + 5 + 6 + 7 = 22 = 4 = 1$$
$$7 + 8 + 9 + 10 = 34 = 7 = 1$$
$$10 + 11 + 12 + 13 = 46 = 10 = 1$$
every four digits added together are akin in vibration frequency to "One".

Through ALL planes and dimensions of existence . . . **Y H V H** is there, showing us that **God is the family**; unions of integrated, integral individuals, being as one.

In other words . . . sisters and brothers . . . the "Word", **Y H V H,** has been given forth so that you will know – without doubt – that God (the Eternal Being of Wisdom and Love) is in you, and all around you, at the same time. Having the intrinsic power of it's meaning, sounding and viewing embedded in its letters, it can bestow

"Illumination" and a mental re-unifying, by your simply accepting to know and **use** it. As we said at the beginning, Aquarius is the age of "I know"

So . . . NOW **it's time to** KNOW !

The Name YAHOWHA was revealed to the enslaved Hebrew people and set them free because they were willing to **accept and live** the highest moral and intellectual standards of living for that time, "THE 10 COMMANDMENTS" ! This set the "tone" for the astrological age of that time, Aries.

Because the human race – 3500 years ago – could largely not read or write, this left the Hebrew people (with 100% literacy, while a united nation) head and shoulders above the people of other nations, intellectually. However . . . with the receiving of this Name came the admonition of the withholding of it's utterance. So, when the great prophet received It and asked, " Who shall I say has sent me?", he was told to tell them . . . "I AM THAT I AM" – which really means the same thing as YHVH ! The true meaning is . . . "WHAT YOU ARE . . . GOD IS . . . AND WHAT GOD IS . . . YOU ARE" !   The

Hebrews called this "The lesser face and the greater face". The ancient Greeks called this the microcosm and the macrocosm.

Now here is another insight. The Hebrew for I AM THAT I AM can also be translated to mean: "I WILL BE AS I WILL TO BE". This indicates that – when you, the individual, know **"YHVH** with all your heart and soul and might" – you too can attain the freedom and power to know and determine your own future ! Not many of us can do this now, but – as our "Earthly Spiritual Father" would say: "The journey of 1000 miles begins with one step."

The steps are here in "Liberation". The ancient phrase "I AM THAT I AM" (in Hebrew), is made up of 11 letters. Aquarius is the 11th sign. The central letter (Shin) of these 11, is that which represents what is known as "The Holy Spirit" – or Soul Intelligence. When Shin is added in to the center of YHVH, the name of the father then becomes the name of the son, Yahshuah, or YHSVH. The name Yahshuah resonates, numerically, to 11 – like "I Am That I Am", and 11 is a "Master Number".

So, now you can see how this all points to our present "Age of Aquarius" and enlightenment!

All of this knowledge now makes intelligible to us . . . the meaning of the words "I AND MY FATHER ARE ONE" and "IT IS THE FATHER WITHIN THAT DOETH THE WORKS" and "I AM YHVH, YOUR GOD . . . YOU SHALL HAVE NO OTHER GODS BEFORE ME".

How could anything come before "I AM"? One must "Be" before one can "Know". So, therefore, Sisters and Brothers, "UNTO THINE OWN SELF BE TRUE", "KNOW THYSELF", "YHVH" . . . AND "MAY YOUR KNOWING **YHVH** SET YOU FREE"!

How to chant or sing the most ancient name:
Any way you are inspired. You can sing it to a tune you love or make up. Being a 4 lettered word, it has four beats which lends itself to the 4/4 time or to chanting it rhythmically, with a drum.

Our earthly spiritual father included this in his

instruction of the 8th commandment for the Age of Aquarius.

VI – DEATH AND DYING
Commentary

"The Three Worst Things" . . .

- ~ To Wait for One Who Comes Not
- ~ To Try to Please and Please Not
-   ~ To Love One Who Loves Not

The nineteenth century saw the development of spiritualism and a belief that the human personality survived, entirely and unchanged, after death. People witnessed the "Near Death" experiences and these brought "Reincarnation" back to the minds of many, along with the concept of "Karma", which brought the death and dying experience back to a more natural state of acceptance.

Although, dying nowadays can be lonely and impersonal because the patient is often taken out of his familiar environment or home and rushed to an emergency room. He may cry for rest, peace and dignity . . . but he will often get infusions, transfusions and a heart machine ! He may want one single person to stop for one single minute, so he can ask a single question - but he will get a dozen people, round the clock, all busily preoccupied with heart rate, pulse and electrocardiogram functions . . . but not with him, as a human being.

There seem to be five phases of the journey towards death: <u>Denial</u>, which is temporary; <u>Anger,</u> when denial cannot be maintained; <u>Bargaining,</u> an attempt to negotiate for time; <u>Depression</u>, the process of losing everyone and everything and then <u>Acceptance</u>.

The consciousness still has experiences, after separating from the body, so it is important to protect this special timeframe ! As the time of death approaches, the first thing that the dying person experiences is the five elements dissolving into one another, the blood, the body, the muscle, the bones and the breath. From this time forward, there is no turning back . . . the time of death has arrived. It is at this time that mind looks into mind and – if one truly has no fear – liberation of consciousness is attained.

During the next 4 days, one goes through the "River of life" . . . reviewing all, and meeting "The Dweller" of your own making. The Buddha says that, for 49 days after death, a person is still near and present. This is the interval between death and rebirth. When the consciousness leaves the body and we are exiting it, there is a black out . . . then a clear light . . . clarity and emptiness free from birth, death, and location.

Many have visitations from the spiritual realms to help them pass over. "They will gaze up with a continent of radiance," then they are gone. They take no more breaths, but they still have a heart beat . . . usually for about 13 seconds. Then it is over. This is a state of "Grace", as one comes into the "Circumvent Force" of a high, Spiritual energy, welcoming you "Home". They say that - at this point - a person looses 24 grams. The atomic scientists at NASA have said that it is 28 grams.

We should practice during our lifetime to gain the knowledge and experience that will help us at the moment of death. Each day is a river of life to be viewed and corrected . . . called "Death while living". The balance of practicing how to "Live your life rightly" is learning and practicing how to "Die rightly" – with no fear – for, in the end, it comes for everyone.

To keep your loved one at home, in their environment, supported by family and loved ones (with flowers and candles and only positive thoughts and actions) is ultimate and natural. It is a tribal instinct . . . and a Sacred Act . . . but for a long time not considered legal !

Most States, however, now recognize "Religious" beliefs and the rights of families wanting "Natural" home funerals. Various laws have been passed which allow one to have a loved one, after their death, undisturbed for as long as they want – or possibly handle it through a local Funeral Home's "Cold storage". Most European countries already allow this

The Family may view and visit the deceased through out these 3 ½ days, then the burial ceremony of choice is conducted.

VII – AND WHAT MIGHT THIS ALL MEAN TO ME ?

Our "PLANET GODDESS EARTH", is moving into <u>The Age of Aquarius.</u>

Father always taught us that the actual date of transition was
<u>September 17th, 8:00 pm, 2001</u>.

Does this mean that everything changes completely and suddenly ? We shall see ! But if we stop to think about it . . . We COULD just seize this opportunity, to Set a new standard for ourselves . . . Even visualize the creation of a completely new life ! ? !

Jesus saith: "As a man *thinketh* . . . s<u>o</u> shall he *be* !" <u>*Maybe*</u> - just *maybe* – we can <u>*change history*</u> . . . ? ! At least . . . <u>Our own, personal F*ragment* of it</u> ! ? If you choose to see this as a new opportunity . . . what *are you going to do* with yours ?

MAY WE – as <u>individuals</u> . . . and as the band of "Tribes of the Earth" – choose to work together to *<u>engender</u>* a true, "N*<u>ew Age</u>*" . . . of <u>respect, love and joy</u> ! *<u>An age of understanding</u>* . . . Of *<u>each other</u>* ! An age of *<u>true love</u>* ! And *<u>forgiveness</u>* ! *<u>Sincere forgiveness</u>* . . . from the heart . . . *<u>Not only</u>* from the mind !

After all . . . "I am you and you are me . . .
                          So it exits for eternity…"

Is this starting to sound like "Spiritual consciousness" ! ?

Well . . . IT IS ! Are we ready for that ?

For those who feel ready . . . or for <u>anyone</u> who chooses *any* path toward "Ascension" . . . you will be given many "Keys" and you will face many difficult "Tests" ! Should you begin to find "The Path" rocky and steep, just remember . . . "All things come to him who waits !"

Recently one man came forth, who felt that Mankind needed a little extra help, during this major "Right of Passage". He felt that it was about time that Man be given **"The**

Word" ! And he had the courage to speak "The Word". . . teach it . . . even to sing it.

That man became the Father of The Source Family . . . and he recognized the pure God within himself by changing His Own Name to "Ya Ho Wha" !

There are many "Paths". For those who are moved to attempt to find their "Path" . . . He told us that: "The greatest spirit . . . is made manifest at the *physical* plane !"

"You can do anything you want to do . . . As long as you are Kind !"

He taught us that Spiritual growth is much more difficult, if you don't take care of your body . . . your "Vehicle" ! Eat the very best foods that you can ! Live, raw, organic . . . Real food to purify your blood, which sustains your electrical nerve force !

"If your 'Food trip' is together, your 'Spirit trip' is together."

"The very structure, the molecular structure of the body, must be changed and altered to prepare your body for the "Light". This can be very speedy work because - as your science has told you — you completely replace every cell in your body every 7 years." Keep your muscles strong to give your nerve force good tools to work with.

Meditate ! Keep the "Channels" open to allow the free flow of "Universal Life Energy".

Always love and respect each other . . . Your spouse, your children, your family and others.

Men . . . Love and protect your women - For they are literally the "Mothers of all living" !

And — upon waking — say: "Ya Ho Wha . . . Be still and know that I am God."

. . . . And, have fun !

Jesus saith: "As a man *thinketh* . . . So shall he *be*!"

Ya Ho Wha saith . . .
"You create your own reality !
Through the power of your words and . . .
your thought-force visualization !"

"Heaven *is not* a place we die and go to !" **This** is our Heaven ! *Can we choose to create it here on earth ? Can we re~birth ! ? !* This *new* birth . . . Into "The Golden Age" . . .

The promise of the new age is:
"We shall see no more through a glass darkly,
                              but face to face."
The mass of men lead lives of quiet desperation !

What will you do with your "new play" ?

What if *you* said "E*nough* already" ! ? ! *with the* jealousy . . . *stop it*, already . . . *with the* mistrust . . . with *the* doubts of each other's intentions . . . *With the* miscommunications ! ! !
            Can't we move on ! ? !

Our highest manifestation of God on this little Planet, is "The Family" . . . Let us do our best to be good fathers and mothers . . . Loving husbands and wives . . . Brothers and sisters . . . Righteous men and women !

Are we able to open our souls so that we may be transfigured ?

Often . . . "The Spirit is willing, but the flesh is weak !"

Father knew that God was everything, and that nothing could occur that was not God. He had certain knowing that the process of creation, outlined in the Name, would proceed, unerringly and inevitably. The timing — as He always told us — was the only thing we could not predict. And, even now, the timing confounds some . . . but patience rewards her devotees.

We must work to try to see the God in each other, alive and well, and smiling at us. Father preceded us, as our Head. The Wisdom and the Love can only live, if we practice them and share them with others.

Let God live in the Wisdom and the Love that you give.

Lose Memory ~
                            Lose All !

THE FOUR RULES OF THE

"WHITE MAGICIAN"

To will,

    To dare,

        To know,

            To be silent.

"If you want to keep something sacred . . .

        keep it in the silence of your heart."

THE FOUR RULES OF THE DISCIPLE

Before the eyes can see...

    They must be incapable of tears.

Before the ear can hear...

    It must have lost its sensitiveness.

Before the voice can speak
in the presence of the masters...

    It must have lost the power to wound.

Before the soul can stand
in the presence of the masters...

    Its feet must be washed in the blood of the heart!

"THE SEVEN GREAT PRINCIPLES OF TRUTH"

The principles of truth are seven; he who knows these understandingly, possesses the magic key before whom the doors to the temple fly open.

1. <u>Mentalism</u> - the all is mind; the universe is mental.

2. <u>Correspondence</u> - as above so below- as below so above. There is harmony, agreement and correspondence between the several planes of manifestation, life and being.

3. <u>Vibration</u> - nothing rests; everything moves, vibrates and circles. Motion is manifest in everything in the universe.

4. <u>Polarity</u> - all manifested things have two sides, two aspects, and two poles. Everything is dual, everything has its pair of opposite; like and unlike are the same, opposites are identical in nature, but different in degree; extremes meet, all truths are half truths; all paradoxes maybe reconciled.

5. <u>Rhythm</u> - in everything there is a manifested measured motion, a flow and inflow, a pendulum like movement between the two poles manifested on the physical, mental or spiritual planes. Everything

flows in and out, everything has its tides, all things rise and fall; the pendulum swing manifests in everything; the measure of the swing to the right is the measure of the swing to the left; rhythm compensates.

6. <u>Cause and Effect</u> - law pervades the universe, nothing happens by chance. Chance is but a name for law not recognized. Every cause has its effect; every effect has its cause, everything happens according to law, chance is but a name for law not recognized; there are many planes of causation, but nothing escapes the law.

7. <u>Gender</u> - the masculine and feminine principles are ever present and active in all phases of phenomena, on each and every plane of life. Gender is in everything; everything has its masculine and feminine principles, gender manifests on all planes.

~ Hermes Trismegistus the Great; the master of masters

The original Suns and Daughters of Ya Ho Wha have now formed "The Source Foundation" to continue His "Great Work". We endeavor to provide more information and His Teachings for those who are "On The Path", make available his incredible, spontaneous music and we are working to build a meditation center and Home Base for the Family in Hawaii.

For information on the Music & Family ~ please visit The Source Foundation website at:

http://yahowha.org

THE SOURCE FOUNDATION
PO BOX 679
Kilauea, Hawaii 96754
ya_ho_wha@yahowha.org

**Published in cooperation with
 The Source Archives -**
Isis Aquarian
418 Iliwahi Loop
Kailua, Hi 96734
Email isis at: Charlene_yhvh@hotmail.com

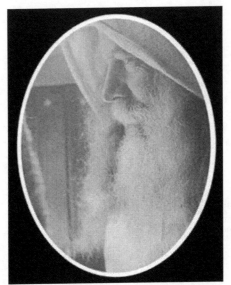
Father Yod ~ 1972

Father ~ 1973

Ya Ho Wha ~ 1975

The Family in LA ~ 1973

Some of the Family at the 2001, Hawaii gathering

FATHER (1922 - 1975)

Made in the USA
Lexington, KY
03 May 2016